The Complete Book of
Superstition, Prophecy, and Luck

The
Complete Book
of
Superstition,
Prophecy
AND Luck

LEONARD R. N. ASHLEY

BARRICADE BOOKS INC.
New York

Published by Barricade Books Inc.
150 Fifth Avenue
New York, NY 10011

Printed in the United States of America.

Library of Congress Cataloging-in-Publication Data

Ashley, Leonard R.N.
[Wonderful world of superstition, prophecy and luck]
The complete book of superstition, prophecy and luck /
Leonard R.N. Ashley.
p. cm
Originally published: The wonderful world of superstition,
prophecy, and luck. New York: Dembner, c1984.
Includes index.
ISBN 1-56980-050-2 (pbk)
1. Superstition. 2. Folklore. 3. Prophecies (Occultism) 4. Fortune. I. Title.
BF1775.A74 1995
001.9'6—dc20   95-32693
CIP

First printing

For Raymond William Ayre
si placeo, tuum est

Contents

Foreword

A great American humorist once said that it ain't what we don't know that hurts us, it's all the things we do know that *ain't true*.

For example, most people are absolutely convinced that hot water will freeze faster than cold water. Under certain special circumstances—outdoors in Alaska in a styrofoam cup—this is true. In your freezer it is not, so if you put hot water into your ice trays, don't expect it to make ice faster than cold water does.

This makes an interesting point about belief in the supernatural—in any and all of its many colorful forms. The striking aspect of *hot* water *freezing* and freezing *faster than cold* makes it stick in the mind, and we greatly enjoy the unusualness of the idea. This accounts for ignorant and irrational belief in many of the phenomena in this book—the stubborn insistence of people in believing in the fantastical even when it has been proved that it *ain't true*. Faith welcomes miracles.

Superstition is a sort of faith. In *De divinatione*, Cicero said that superstition is a parody of religion, that it poisons and destroys all peace of mind. Edmund Burke called it "the religion of feeble minds." Wrote Francis Bacon:

Such is the way of all superstition, whether in astrology, dreams, omens, divine judgments, or the like; wherein men, having a delight in such vanities, mark the events where they are fulfilled, but where they fail, though they happen much oftener, neglect and pass them by.

Nonetheless, occult matters are colorful and men do have "a delight in such vanities," and that is what this book is about. The first half is devoted largely to folk beliefs: the people's magic, charms and incantations and cures and omens and wonder working carried out by ordinary people according to their own rules. The second half takes up "educated" forms of the occult: pseudo sciences developed and practiced and studied by learned men down through the ages. Both kinds of superstition have their adherents; both have their skeptics. Both are interesting for what they reveal of human nature.

But this is, above all, a book to be enjoyed. So scoff at our ignorant and wildly imaginative ancestors. Or pause before some item of folk wisdom here and wonder if perhaps there may not, after all, be something in it. . . . Whatever suits you best.

And if you happen to hit upon something equally intriguing that I have omitted, why not write to me and tell me about it? I cannot undertake to answer all your letters, but I shall read them with interest. Now, good reading. And good luck.

L. R. N. A.

PART ONE

Superstition

"Crush the Infamous Thing!"

THAT is the great Voltaire's remark regarding superstition, for Voltaire lived in—was the embodiment of—the Age of Enlightenment, and thinkers of his day attempted to apply rationality not only to political and social life but to religion and morality as well. Superstition links causes and effects in ways that defy logic and fail all impartial tests, and thus superstition was at odds with the new scientific way of thinking dominant in Voltaire's time.

Nonetheless, superstition is ineradicable, Frederick the Great assured the philosopher. Superstition has always existed and has formed both the

1

alpha and the omega of religions: the primitive beliefs from which they emerge and the baroque delusions into which they finally fall.

In reality, superstition is the enemy of true religion, as many religious leaders have said. In 1080, for instance, in the very beginning of those Middle Ages so often pointed to as the heyday of superstition, Pope Gregory VII wrote to King Harold the Simpleminded of Denmark to warn him unequivocally that blaming tempests, illness, and other afflictions on witches was heresy. These, he said, were Acts of God, and to punish witches for them was only to injure the innocent and further provoke the wrath of the deity.

There are many people alive today who are far less "modern" and enlightened than Pope Gregory was a thousand years ago. We are often as much in a "dark age" now as our ancestors were in the Middle Ages.

Mankind clings to its superstitions in the face of all intellectual advance, all evidence to the contrary. Mankind has a will to ignore evidence that contradicts its treasured beliefs. Mankind does not want to find out it has been wrong. It searches for ways of holding onto the comfortable, even if incorrect, explanations of the past. One coincidence can make a convert; all instances to the contrary just don't count.

We all have some superstitions, of course, because we are all carrying some of the baggage of the past. No one can be rational and informed all the time. Nobody can be entirely free of ancient fears, or of foolish fancies. Many of the beliefs that follow will seem outrageously silly. Others, however improbable they sound, may draw more on practical experience than we are aware of. Still others may appeal to some romantic streak lurking unrealized in our prosaic modern souls. It is hoped that all readers will recognize at least *some* of what comes next. Knock on wood!

1
People

SHADOWS

The ancients believed that a man's shadow and his reflection in some measure represented his soul. Hence, in legends, vampires and other soulless entities cast no shadow and cannot be seen in mirrors. Hence, too, the ancient tale of the man who sold his shadow to the Devil and the Richard Strauss opera about a supernatural wife, *Die Frau ohne Schatten* (*The Woman Without a Shadow*).

Many people believe that to see one's shadow cast by the moon is bad luck. On the other hand shadows can be used to ward off evil, as is shown by the superstitious natives of Transylvania who in the eighteenth century tried to build a shadow into a wall.

Some Jews believe that if a man cannot see his shadow at nightfall on the seventh day of the feast of Sukkoth, Hoshana Rabbah, he will die within a year. Likewise, in ancient Greece, it was believed that any unauthorized person who entered the sanctuary of Zeus on Mount Lycaeus would lose his shadow and die within a year.

Many different peoples hold the folk belief that injury done to a shadow will inflict the living body to a similar degree. The aborigines of Australia sometimes stab an enemy's shadow as a way of attacking the man; and when they are working magic against an enemy they are careful not to allow their own shadows to fall on the spell object, for fear the curse will turn back upon themselves.

Some Arabs believe that if a hyena steps on a man's shadow, it will deprive the man of speech. A dog could do the same thing to a hyena by

3

stepping on *its* shadow. On the other hand, if a dog were standing on a roof so that its shadow fell on the ground and a passing hyena stepped on it, the dog would be jerked to the ground as if by a rope.

One of the best-known shadow beliefs is that a shadow helps the groundhog (the badger in England) predict the weather. The animal is thought to emerge from hibernation on February 2, and if he sees his shadow—that is, if the day is sunny— he returns to his den, and there will be six more weeks of winter. Headquarters for this prediction is the town of Punxsutawney, Pennsylvania, about seventy miles northeast of Pittsburgh, where the Groundhog Club is located. The superstition is based, however, on an ancient tradition associated with the feast of Candlemas, celebrated on February 2. "If Candlemas Day is bright and clear," men said, "there'll be two winters in the year."

LADDERS

It is dangerous to walk under a ladder, but it is also dangerous to walk on a ladder lying on the ground. If you step over the ladder while making a wish, your wish will come true. In fact, you can walk under a ladder and still be lucky if you cross yourself or cross your fingers and make a wish first.

If a woman walks under a ladder, it's the same as if she sits on a table: She will not get married for at least a year.

CIDER

Makers of homemade cider have many superstitions about the brew. It must be made while the moon is waning or the apples will shrivel up and the cider be sour. There are all sorts of theories about how to make scrumpy or some other drink "work," how much sugar or honey or whatever to add, how adding a few parsnips or beets gives it something to "feed on," and so on. Some country people add half a horseshoe to the cider barrel to "put iron in it." They maintain that when the cider is "done," the metal will be found to have disappeared. (Similarly, some people drop a dime into a churn to make the butter "come.")

DOUBLES

Multiple births have awakened feelings of awe and wonder among many different peoples. Even the statistics are curious. In the United States (and based on statistics collected before the advent of fertility pills), according to the *Encyclopaedia Britannica* there are eighty-six single births for every set of twins, eighty-six sets of twins for every set of triplets, and eighty-six sets of triplets for every set of quadruplets. It is hardly surprising, therefore, that superstitions about twins abound. They go back to the Gemini, and beyond.

The commonest superstition in this connection is some variation on the theme of the Corsican brothers—the idea that twins can somehow feel what happens to each other, even at a distance, that they are really one soul in two bodies. Often, too, it seems that one twin is doubly disturbed and even feels guilty when the other dies.

Many Europeans believe in the *Döppelganger* (double) who looks just like the original but seems to lead an independent existence. Reports are heard from time to time of one man being recognized by friends at the same time in two widely separated places. The record for such multiple appearances is probably held by one Johannes Teutonicus, who one day in 1221 was seen celebrating Mass at Mainz, Halberstadt, and Cologne, all at the same hour. Fortunately these *Döppelgangen* did not meet, for Germans believe that if a man meets his double face to face, he will die.

Similarly the Yoruba of West Africa and the Baganda of Uganda believe that every man has a spirit double, a twin brother or sister, in effect, whose destiny is intricately bound up with his own. Perhaps it has something to do with the high incidence of twins among the Yoruba, much higher than the above-mentioned American rate. It is sad to note that the commonest of all the beautiful Yoruba cult carvings are those to commemorate twins who die in infancy.

HAIR TODAY . . .

Hair has long been a symbol of sexuality, and this has given rise to a number of religious practices concerning it. In times past, nuns, when they took their vows, and Orthodox Jewish women, when they married, shaved their heads and adopted wimples and wigs instead. Sikh men to this day are forbidden to cut their hair and instead bind it up elaborately and hide it under turbans. This practice recently caused some consternation among British motor-safety experts when it was discovered that the crash helmets prescribed for motorcyclists would not fit over the turbans, and the Sikhs refused to abandon the turbans. Eventually Sikh motorcyclists were exempted from the law.

Samson in the Bible seems to have belonged to a religious sect that forbade the cutting of hair. When Delilah cut it for him, it cost him his strength—probably symbolizing the loss of the faith that had formerly upheld him. Today the beards and side curls still worn by some Orthodox Jews are a survival of this religious practice.

In ancient Egypt, pharaohs shaved their chins and then wore fake beards for ceremonial occasions. The Egyptians made no bones about the fact that it was fake; the strap attaching it is plainly shown in portrait statues of these kings. Such a fake beard was even worn by a queen of Egypt, the famous Hatshepsut.

Sidi Mohammed ben Aissa (1456–1533) was a Moroccan holy man who, believing he could study best by night, stayed up all night to read the Koran. To keep himself awake, he tied a lock of his hair to the wall. If he nodded, the pain brought him sharply to attention. Today, his followers, of the Aissawa (or Isawa) sect, wear a long lock in his memory.

Other Muslims wear a single long lock of hair in the belief, it is said, that they will be drawn up to heaven by the hair at the hour of their death. The long tassle on the fez represents this lock of hair.

Hair figures to some extent in customs. Lovers used to keep a lock of the loved one's hair in a locket or the back of a watch, and locks of hair from famous heads are much-valued treasures. (Napoleon in particular was always being asked for souvenir locks, and many of these are still extant.) About the time of the Civil War, "hair pictures" were in vogue—hair wound around bits of wire and bent into the shape of some image, usually a flower. The Confederate Museum in Richmond, Virginia, has a framed bouquet of hair flowers, every "petal" of which is composed of hair from a different Confederate hero.

Naturally hair has given rise to a number of superstitions.

Curly hair is lucky. You can make it curly by eating bread crusts (and carrots and spinach and prunes and virtually anything else that Mother wants her recalcitrant child to finish up).

To "put hair on your chest," eat substantial food, such as meat and potatoes.

Masturbation was once thought to make your palms hairy (a bestial act leading to a bestial appearance was the rationale, obviously).

To make your hair grow longer, brush it a hundred times a day. Rain is also supposed to make your hair grow. So is frequent cutting.

Sailors used to wear tarred pigtails, as protection against back-of-the-neck blows—from cutlasses in battle and from falling spars in peacetime. The apronlike collar of a "sailor suit" was supposed to protect the jacket from the tar on the pigtail. But when sailors did have their hair cut, they preferred to have it done during a storm at sea, which was widely believed to be lucky.

If a hairpin falls out of your hair, a friend is thinking of you. If you lose it, you will make an enemy. If you find a hairpin—as when you find a needle or pin—you must pick it up or you will have bad luck. For best results, hang it on a hook.

If a man has his hair cut when the moon is waning, his hair will dwindle too.

If you eat a raven's egg, it will turn your hair black, and if you suffer a severe fright, it will turn your hair white overnight.

Many people believe hair fibers are extremely fragile—hence, "to hang by a hair," meaning "to be on the verge of falling." Actually, hair is stronger than it looks, having a good half the tensile strength of steel.

Many sports figures, finding themselves in a winning/losing streak will vow not to shave until the streak comes to an end. Winners don't want to take chances with good luck, and losers hope to push themselves on to do better.

LIGHTNING

Lightning no longer impresses most people as evidence of God's wrath, but that does not mean they have abandoned superstitions concerning it.

The commonest belief is that lightning never strikes twice in the same place. This is not true, of course; skyscrapers are repeatedly struck by lightning, and *Life* magazine once published a photographic story showing the Empire State Building being struck six or seven times in one year alone. But many people still believe the old superstition.

To protect yourself from lightning, wrap yourself in a feather bed, sleep with a steel thimble under your pillow, or equip your house with a piece of hawthorn wood cut on Holy Thursday. In Britain they hold that if you can find a piece of coal under a mugwort plant at noon or midnight on

Midsummer Day (June 24), it will prevent you from being struck. In Germany brands from the Easter bonfire serve the same purpose.

On the other hand, in the American West it is believed that where lightning strikes, you'll find oil.

THE SUPERSTITIONS OF KIDS

If you see a red truck: "Red truck, good luck." For good luck, put a penny in your shoe. When you see a ladybug, pick it up gently, put it on your hand, and for good luck encourage it to fly away, saying, "Ladybug, Ladybug, fly away home. Your house is on fire and your children alone."

If you see a white horse, *stamp* it: lick your right thumb, touch it to the palm of your left hand, "paste it down" with a good blow from the right fist.

If you see an eyelash on someone's cheek, have them make a wish and guess whether it's on the right or the left. If they guess right, the wish will come true.

When it rains say: "Rain, rain, go away. Come again another day."

If you make a face at the clock as it strikes twelve, your face may stay that way.

If you see a ghost or a bogeyman, say: "Crisscross, double-cross. Tell the monster to get lost."

To find out if your sweetheart likes you, the way you like her, pull the petals off a daisy one by one, reciting, "She loves me, she loves me not." Whichever it ends up on is the right answer. (Daisies usually have an odd number of petals.) Or you count apple seeds as you recite:

> One I love, two I love, three I love, I say.
> Four I love with all my heart, five I'll cast away.
> Six he loves, seven she loves, eight they both love.
> Nine he comes, ten he tarries,
> Eleven he courts and twelve he marries.

If you tell a lie, cross your fingers behind your back. If you tell the truth, wet your index finger in your mouth, take it out and say:

> Is my finger wet?
> Is my finger dry?
> Cross my heart and hope to die.

Blowing out the candles on a birthday cake in one breath will make your wish come true. Hitting a baseball with the label on the bat will split the bat. Stepping on a crack in the sidewalk will cause something awful to happen to your mother.

FIRE

Man has known how to light and use fire since Neanderthal times. The magic powers of a fire were vital to early religion, and belief in them survives today in the form of much superstition.

If the fire draws badly, the Devil must be at hand; to counteract him, place the poker upright against the bars—iron crosspieces enclosing the grate—thus forming a cross. If, after poking, the fire burns brightly, it means an absent loved one is in good spirits.

Oblong hollow cinders are called coffins in England, and if one flies out of the fire, it is thought that a death in the family is imminent. A coming birth is indicated by a cradle—an oval cinder—doing the same thing. In America, a hot cinder popping out of the fire means a guest is coming.

In New England, they believe that if a house burns down, another should not be built on the same spot. A fire in your dreams means that you will soon have a quarrel with someone. But hang an adder's skin in the rafters and your house will never catch fire. Or stand branches of dried seaweed on your mantel to obtain the same result.

On my mantelpiece I have Staffordshire china dogs, which are supposed to guard the fire. In ancient times, the same chore was assigned to the old-fashioned iron fire dogs that supported the logs in a fireplace. Human-figure andirons had no magical purpose; they were just there to fool burglars, who might glance in and be deterred by seeing "people" in the room.

In Torres Strait, New Guinea, however, the figure by the fire has a magical task. Made of stone and resembling an old woman, the figure is superstitiously believed to keep an eye on the fire and prevent it from going out.

WARDING OFF EVIL

The Chinese believe that spirits can travel only in straight lines, so they build zigzag bridges to thwart them. A similar Western belief is that witches cannot cross running water, a fact that saved the life of Robert Burns's fictional hero Tam O'Shanter, who reached the River Doon just in time to escape from pursuing witch Cutty Sark.

Another Western way to stop a ghost is the direct approach. Ask it boldly, "What do you want?" It is then supposed to disappear forever.

In ancient Babylonia, men got rid of demons by making small figures of them, placing these figures in tiny boats, and pushing them out into open water, meanwhile pronouncing a magic formula in hopes the boat would capsize.

Many modern habits are the result of still surviving superstitions and the attempt to change ill chance to good.

If you and another person happen to say the same thing at the same time, link little fingers. If someone gives you a knife, give him a coin in return or the knife will "cut" the friendship. The same thing goes for a pair of scissors—or the donor can drop the scissors and step on them as you drop a penny and step on it.

If you stumble, snap your fingers. If the stumble takes place while crossing someone else's threshold (which used to be taken as a sign that you practiced witchcraft), you must immediately turn around three times and say, "I turn myself three times about, And thus I put bad luck to rout."

In the RAF during World War II, a pilot would pick up a pebble from the airfield before takeoff and put it in the pocket of his flying suit; when he returned from his mission, he put it back. Failure to follow this custom was regarded as a sign that you did not expect to get home. (In one squadron it was the custom, when a pilot did fail to return, for his best friend to take two pebbles along on the next mission, to "make up" for the missing man.) It was also an RAF custom to leave some task unfinished or a letter half-written and to give one's wallet to a friend to hold.

SERVANTS' SUPERSTITIONS

The servants in British houses had a great number of folk beliefs and superstitions. They thought, for instance, that it was bad luck to
enter a house for a job before midday.
cross knives at the table.
let water that had been boiled stand cold in a bedroom.
sweep out a bedroom within an hour of a guest's departure.

return a softboiled egg's shell to the kitchen if the bottom had not been bashed in with a spoon.

start a new job on a Friday.

UP AND AT 'EM

Getting out of bed on the wrong side can ruin your day. What's the right side? The right side is the right side—because the left side is *sinister* (Latin for "left"). In many hotel rooms, if a wall is handy, the bed's left side is placed against it so that the sleeper cannot make a mistake.

Some authorities say you must get out the same side you got in, "otherwise the interrupted 'circle' also suggests symbolically a bad or unpleasant day." Never attempt to avoid difficulties by climbing over the footboard to get into bed. That's extremely bad luck.

ACTORS AND THE STAGE

No aspect of human life has more superstitious people than the performing arts. Luciano Pavorotti always looks for a bent nail on stage before he feels secure singing in opera. John Ford liked to direct films in his "lucky" hat. The Schuberts always tried to avoid opening on an "unlucky" Monday. Walter Hampden, the American Shakespearean, would never speak to other actors backstage while playing Shakespeare.

Many modern actors hold onto ancient folk traditions of the Profession. Here are some of them:

Never whistle in a dressing room.

Never put a hat on a bed or shoes on a table.

Never quote from *Macbeth* or *Hamlet* in conversation or repeat the last line of play dialogue at rehearsal.

Never use real flowers on stage or accept real flowers over the footlights.

Never have lilies or peacock feathers around—perhaps a stage version of antipathy to the Evil Eye.

Never have yellow in a set or green in a costume if it is at all avoidable.

A cane is lucky, but crutches are unlucky onstage.

Knitting on stage is unlucky.

Never remove a wedding ring to go onstage. If a ring is not right for the part you are playing, keep it on, tape over it, and use makeup to disguise the tape.

Never mention the precise number of lines you have in a show, or you'll forget some.

Never open an umbrella on stage.

Never read congratulatory telegrams until after the final curtain on opening night.

Never write on the mirror in your dressing room until after the first performance.

Never send out your laundry until after opening night.

Wigs are unlucky, squeaky shoes lucky.

If the play is a hit, continue to wear the same costume with which you opened. Repair worn places if necessary, but do not change, or the play will lose its appeal.

Call it "Shakespeare's Scottish play," and never say *Macbeth*.

Trip on your first entrance and you'll be lucky.

Don't peek out through the curtain to check the house before a performance.

Bill the straight man over the comedian in a comedy duo.

Spit into your dancing shoes before putting them on.

Never say "Good luck" to a performer. Say "Break a leg!"

TOOTH AND NAIL

Superstitions concerning these parts of the body—the teeth and the toe- and finger-nails—are rife throughout the world.

Wide-apart teeth are a good-luck sign. You will travel widely (especially if it's the front teeth that are gapped), prosper, and be happy.

The first baby tooth that falls out should be either burned in the fire or thrown to the squirrels, with an order for them to provide the child with stronger (permanent) teeth.

If the baby's teeth come early, they claim in the North of England, there will soon be fresh toes—meaning a new baby is on the way.

In Britain, if the child's first tooth appears in the upper jaw, it is believed that he will die in infancy. Among the Azande of Africa such a child is called *irakörinde*, "he who has bad teeth," and he is believed to bring bad luck to the crops. They ask him not to eat the first fruits of the harvest, especially peanuts and corn, lest the rest of it be ruined. In Central Asia, in times past, such a child would be taken out and "exposed"—that is, allowed to die or become the victim of a wild animal.

We also have superstitions about fingernails. Almost universal is the fear of allowing nail clippings to fall into someone else's hands, for this will enable an enemy to work magic against you.

If fingernails are broad, it indicates generosity; if long, lack of thrift; if short, that you are a liar. (Specks on them indicate the number of lies).

A whole mystique has developed about when and how to cut nails. If a child's nails are cut before it is a year old, it will grow up to be a thief. (Many mothers, to avoid this fate, bite off their children's nails.) If a sick person's nails are cut, he will never get well. It's bad luck to cut anybody's nails on a Friday or a Sunday. Many cautious people go by the following jingle.

> Cut them on Monday, cut them for wealth;
> Cut them on Tuesday, cut them for health;
> Cut them on Wednesday, cut them for news;
> Cut them on Thursday, a new pair of shoes;
> Cut them on Friday, cut them for woe;
> Cut them on Saturday, a journey to go;
> Cut them on Sunday, cut them for evil,
> And be all the week as cross as the Devil.

WEATHER OR NOT . . .

Mark Twain was wrong—people *do* do something about the weather. Or try to. Here are some popular folk suggestions.

To bring rain: stick a spade in the ground or kill a spider or burn ferns or heather or carry a statue of your favorite saint to a nearby stream and dunk it.

To hold off rain: carry an umbrella or wash your car or water a parched lawn—preparing for rain scares it off.

But most folk beliefs concerning weather involve predicting it.

Signs of rain: Frogs croaking during the day. A halo around the moon. Smoke sticking close to the ground. A greenish sky at the horizon. Spiders deserting their webs. Swallows flying low. Chickweed closing up. Moles casting up their hills. Horses gathering in the corners of fields. Gulls flying inland. Asses braying and shaking their ears. (Almost any kind of excitement or unusual activity among animals is held to be a prediction of a coming storm.) In New England they also say:

Rain before seven,
Clear before 'leven;
Sun at seven,
Rain at 'leven.

Signs of a severe winter: Heavy coats on foxes. Large nut harvest. Skunks coming in early from the woods to make winter homes in barns. Corn husks difficult to pull apart. Oysters bedding deep. Heavy migration of wild geese. Bees laying up large stores of honey. Another New England proverb:

Onion's skin very thin
Mild winter coming in.
Onion's skin thick and tough
Coming winter cold and rough.

Signs of fair weather: Swallows flying high and rooks nesting high in trees. Ants piling up hills early in the morning. Cattle chasing one another about the pasture. Cobwebs on the grass in the morning. Dandelions opening their petals early. Another proverbial jingle:

Red in the morning,
Sailors take warning;
Red at night,
Sailors delight.

SOME AMERICAN SUPERSTITIONS

Never start any enterprise on a Tuesday. Monday is unlucky. Wednesday is the day for weddings.

If three persons are photographed together, the one in the middle will die first.

Don't sleep with your head pointing north or death will follow.

To keep witches from moving, throw salt under their chairs.

Catch a falling leaf, and you will have twelve months of happiness.

It is bad luck to make a new opening in an old house, to wash a garment before it is worn, to comb your hair after dark, to count stars or graves, to drop a book and not step on it, to see a pin and not pick it up, to bring eggs into the house after sunset or sweep the floor before sunrise, to rock an empty chair or to spin a chair on one leg, to sneeze on a Friday or at the dinner table, to get married on a cloudy day or to stumble as you enter your new home as a bride (hence, the husband carrying his bride across the threshold).

SOME BRITISH SUPERSTITIONS

Not to be outdone by their transatlantic cousins—indeed, many American superstitions came to this continent on the *Mayflower* and its successors—the British also have much time-tested folk wisdom. It varies from region to region. Thus:

Anyone appearing in new clothes must be pinched for good luck (North Country).

When an unmarried young person dies, a Maiden's Crown (for bachelors as well as spinsters) should be hung up in the church (Hampshire).

Skipping rope to make the crops grow used to be common but now is seen only on Good Friday at the Rose Cottage, an inn in Alciston (Sussex).

Thursday has one unlucky hour, the hour before the sun rises (Devonshire).

It is good luck to encounter a deformed or retarded person while going fishing (Shetlands).

When you move into a new house, you must carry a loaf of bread and a plate of salt into every room (North Yorkshire).

To give your lover a handkerchief as a gift means that you will soon part. That's just one example of a folk belief widely held throughout Britain.

PINS

Pins, used to attach one thing to another, seem to have intrigued many people, for there are many superstitions concerning them. Both the English and Americans know the old verse:

> See a pin, pick it up;
> All the day, you'll have good luck.
> See a pin, let it lay;
> Bad luck you'll have all that day.

Others say, "Pick up a pin, pick up sorrow," or "Pass up a pin, pass up a friend."

If the point is toward you, don't pick it up at all. If the head is toward you, however, pick it up by the head. In New England this means you will soon be offered a ride.

Never lend a pin. In the North of England, they say, "You can have it—it's a gift. But I'm not lending it."

Brides should never wear pins as part of their wedding outfit, and if there are some on it, they must be thrown away. If a pin is given to a bridesmaid, it means she will not be married before Whitsuntide (the season of Pentecost, usually late May to early June).

Pins were often employed in black magic, usually to stick into a wax image of some person—either to cause him to sicken and pine (the pain would appear in that part of his body that corresponds to the position of the pin) or to draw one's lover to one's side. Devon sailors carried pincushions for good luck. Some practicing witches wore on their persons bags or pads (usually heart-shaped) into which they stuck pins as a way of doing harm to others. "I'll stick in a pin for you" was a potent threat.

If a pin falls and sticks upright, it means a stranger is coming. For good luck, stick a pin in the lapel of someone's coat. To ward off evil, stick an onion or a sheep's heart full of pins. If you want to keep witches from coming down the chimney, hang the pin-stuck object in the flue.

COINS

A lot of superstition is involved with how to get or hold onto money, but for the moment let's speak of the coins themselves.

Some people consider it lucky to carry a coin bearing the date of their birth or some other significant event in their lives. A purse should never be allowed to be entirely emptied of coins; keep at least one in it for good luck. Likewise, never give a purse or wallet as a gift without including a coin of some denomination.

Turning up a coin with the plow is unlucky; spit on both sides of it.

The luckiest coins of all are those that are bent or have a hole in them, especially if they come to you naturally as part of your change. If you have such a coin, carry or wear it on the left side or hang it around your neck. The Chinese used to mint coins with square holes already in them, representing (in the Chinese view of the cosmos) the round sea and the square earth.

Throwing a coin to a wayside beggar brings good luck. So does tossing a coin into a fountain—a belief so widely held that virtually every well, pond, fountain, and reflecting pool available to the public quickly becomes carpeted with tossed coins. At the U. S. Naval Academy, Annapolis, Maryland, middies toss coins at the statue of Tecumseh, for good luck in exams and at sports.

In Greek mythology, the River Styx had to be crossed to get to the Underworld, and the fare, paid to the ferryman Charon, was one obol (a coin of quite a small amount, although not the very smallest). Before a corpse was buried, relatives placed an obol in its mouth.

In England and throughout Europe, coins were placed on the closed eyes of a corpse and buried with it. In the Balkans, there is a superstition that these coins can render a husband "blind" to his wife's extramarital carryings-on; just take them from the corpse, wash them in wine, and induce the cuckolded husband to drink the wine.

GEM STONES

Rubies make excellent amulets, but are said to work best for those born under the sign of Cancer. They bring peace of mind and prevent all evil and impure thoughts. Since they were believed to be strong protectors of chastity, they were often worn by priests in the Middle Ages. On the other hand, being the color of blood, they also attract werewolves.

Jasper will cure madness. If worn as an amulet with certain cabalistic inscriptions, it is supposed to strengthen the intellect.

Agate is supposed to be beneficial to the eyes and acts as an antidote to the poison of spiders and scorpions.

Bloodstone, a variety of chalcedony, is also called heliotrope. In the Middle Ages it was believed that if the stone heliotrope were combined with the flower heliotrope, it would render a man invisible.

Sapphires were thought to make their owner devout, disposed toward peace, and "cool from inward heat." It also helped him sleep.

Emeralds were believed to be found in the nests of griffins (fabulous beasts, half lion, half eagle). Emeralds bestowed on their owner a good understanding, an excellent memory, and riches. If held under the tongue, an emerald enabled a man to prophesy.

Coral, which the ancient naturalist Pliny thought was a plant, was supposed to be able to stanch blood. Like the emerald and the jasper, coral made a man wise. Babies were given it for teething. It was also supposed to be a good preventive against tempests and floods.

Each month of the calendar has its particular birthstone, supposed to be lucky for the person born in that month. Both Englishmen and Americans seem to be agreed on the following list:

January, garnet.

February, amethyst (good for preventing drunkenness).

March, bloodstone or aquamarine.

April, diamond (if held to the left side, it will ward off enemies, madness, wild and venomous beasts, and chiding and brawling).

May, emerald.

June, agate, pearl, or moonstone (pearls are considered unlucky, especially for engagement rings; they bring tears to the marriage).

July, ruby.

August, sardonyx.

September, sapphire.

October, opal (lucky for all those of October birth, but disastrous for others; an opal ring is reputed to have caused the deaths of Alphonso XII of Spain [1857–88], his wife, his sister, and his sister-in-law).

November, topaz (good to ward off grief and "lunatic passion").

December, turquoise.

BABY SUPERSTITIONS

A baby born with teeth may be a vampire.

A baby born with a caul (the inner fetal membrane or amnion) will be lucky.

A baby with large ears will be generous; one with small ears will be stingy. A baby with a big mouth will be a singer or orator; one with a small mouth will be mean.

It is a good sign if the baby cries at baptism, but it is unlucky to change the baby's name after it has been baptised.

If a baby will not take a coin when it is offered, it will grow up reckless with money. Offer a baby a choice of several objects belonging to different family members, living and dead, and its choice will show you whom it will "take after."

To prevent colic, give the baby hot water that has been poured into a shoe.

To keep the baby well, put it out in the first April shower, put a rabbit's foot in its crib, a bag of sulfur around its neck, or sulfur in its shoes.

To bring luck to a newborn, spit on it or rub it all over with lard.

If a baby is born feet first, rub bay leaves on its legs within its first few hours of life. Otherwise it will grow up lame or be lamed in an accident.

Never let an infant see itself in a mirror before it is several months old, or it will die within the year.

Never rock an empty cradle, or the baby to which it belongs will have an early death.

A GRAIN OF SALT

Salt has been recognized, since ancient times, as highly significant in the life of man. Ancient peoples employed it in acts of religious worship. The Greeks burned salt and flesh on their altars. Catholics add salt to water before it is blessed and rendered into holy water (a sacramental and a means of grace).

Superstitions about salt abound also. It is bad luck to spill it. If this should happen, throw a pinch over your left shoulder (where the Devil lurks) as a propitiation.

Salt is the first item to be placed on the dinner table when it is being set, the last thing removed. Concerning salt at the table, there's an old American saying, "Pass me salt, pass me sorrow," and its English version: "Help to salt, help to sorrow."

A pinch of salt was dropped into a churn, so that the butter would "come."

Because salt preserved food, it was thought to purify. In Scotland and Ireland they put salt on the chest of a corpse—up to three handfuls. In the North of England, a young baby, leaving the house for the first time, is given salt—plus an egg, some money, and a piece of bread—so that he will never want for the necessities of life. Similarly, in many parts of the world an arriving stranger is greeted at the threshold of the house with bread and salt.

"ALWAYS A BRIDESMAID . . ."

A comic song of the British music halls used to describe the plight of the bridesmaid who discovered that "wedding bells" were always ringing "for someone else." Being a bridesmaid carries various superstitions of its own, many of them concerned with that very problem—finding a groom of one's own.

To stumble while walking down the aisle is very bad luck, probably leading to old-maidhood. To be a bridesmaid three times used to guarantee that one will never be a bride. Then someone decided that being a bridesmaid *seven* times would break the jinx.

The best way to be sure that you will be the next bride is to catch the bride's bouquet when it is thrown. (In France, a garter is thrown rather than the bouquet.) The bride often takes careful aim, however, so if you are not her choice for the one to follow her down the aisle, you may be out of luck.

If a bridesmaid puts a piece of wedding cake under her pillow, she will dream of her future husband. If a bridesmaid's chances seem really slim in the marrying line, a bride can give her the shoes she wore at the wedding, and these should have been old shoes, anyway. A bride's shoes are a potent charm.

DON'TS

If you want to avoid bad luck, DON'T
    count the stars.
    comb your hair after dark.
    burn apple branches for firewood.
    bring a wild bird into the house.
    dream of cabbages.
    wash new clothes before wearing them.
    make a new opening in an old house.
    watch a person going until they disappear entirely.
    see a crow.
    have your fruit trees bloom twice in a year.
    have your sweet potatoes bloom at all.
    plant a weeping willow.
    have a bat land on your head or touch it.
    take your cat with you when you move.
    get the ASPCA after me for telling you that last one.

2
Animals and Plants

A ROSE IS A ROSE

The national badge of England is the Tudor rose, a popular heraldic device in many coats of arms. The rose is associated with Aphrodite and considered by Christians to be the Virgin's own flower. Yet the rose is often regarded as an unlucky flower.

If roses bloom in the fall, there will be an epidemic of disease the following year. If the Scotch rose blooms out of season, there will be a shipwreck. It is bad luck to scatter the petals of roses, particularly red roses (associated with blood), on the ground.

On the other hand, it was the custom to plant rose bushes on graves— white for a young virgin, red for a person known for charity. And wild roses placed over the gate to a cow pasture will prevent witches from riding on the backs of cows.

In the language of flowers, roses speak of many things but mostly of love: bridal rose, happy love; burgundy rose, unconscious beauty; cabbage rose, ambassador of love; damask rose, brilliant complexion; deep red rose, bashful shame; dog rose, pleasure and pain; rosa mundi, variety; thornless rose, early attachment.

TOADS

In America it's considered bad luck to kill a toad—a belief perhaps derived from the Indians, because throughout tropical America the natives regard the toad as a benevolent water spirit that watches over and ensures the purity of the water (and hence the harvest).

In England and some other parts of the world, however, toads are often feared and loathed as emissaries of the Devil. It was thought that they carried venom like vipers and that touching them could at least cause warts. A farmer who suspected that someone had "overlooked"—bewitched with the Evil Eye—his cattle, burned a toad alive at midnight. This would force the witch to appear. In West Africa, an epidemic is halted by dragging a toad through the village, then casting it—now having absorbed the plague—into the forest.

Despite general mistrust of the toad, the English clung for many centuries to the notion of a "toad stone." This was thought to be a gem stone located in the head of an aged toad, which could indicate the presence of poison by changing color. In *As You Like It* Shakespeare has the banished Duke say: "The toad, ugly and venomous, Wears yet a precious jewel in his head."

Sir Walter Scott's family possessed something reputed to be a toad stone. (The Wizard of the North was supposed to have been descended from a genuine spell-casting and -removing wizard.) Sir Walter once described the family treasure in a letter to a friend: "a toadstone, a celebrated amulet . . . was sovereign for protecting new-born children and their mothers from the power of fairies, and has been repeatedly borrowed from my mother, on account of this virtue."

TREES

Many popular superstitions attach themselves to certain trees. Poplar leaves tremble, according to folk belief, because it was supposedly on a cross of poplar wood that Christ was crucified. Elder is unlucky, too, says another tale, because it is the tree on which Judas Iscariot hanged himself. Cypress trees, frequently planted in graveyards, especially in those of Eastern Mediterranean countries, are said to offer shelter to the dead during bad weather. Western European churchyards often featured yew trees, and it was considered extremely bad luck to injure a churchyard yew, though branches might be stolen for magic wands.

Apple orchards had to be serenaded, and cider-soaked toast left in the branches of the trees "for the robins" (actually, for the god of the orchard). If a dead animal is not buried under the roots of a newly planted tree, it will not bear fruit. An orchard will do better the next year, they say in the West of England, if children are permitted to steal the apples left on the trees after apple picking ("the piskies' harvest"). One must never take *all* the apples off a tree when picking.

All pruning and grafting of fruit trees must be done at the increase of the moon. Thomas Tusser, a sixteenth-century English writer on agriculture—he wrote his *Husbandrie* entirely in verse—gave this advice to farmers:

> From moon being changed
> Till past be the prime,
> For graffing and cropping
> Is very good time.

Around the world, many trees are said to be the habitations of good and evil spirits and to grant blessings or magical dreams to those who touch them. Greeks believed in Dryads, oak nymphs who inhabited woods and ravines and romped with satyrs. Some people will not touch an unlucky tree and, even when cutting down a tree, will first ask forgiveness of the spirit who lives in it.

In Darjeeling, India, there is a sacred tree of Poona. Some years ago an old woman named Shelibai ran around it a million times to ensure the birth of a grandson. When the boy was born, the news took three months to reach the grandmother, so she made 200,000 laps too many.

The Mogul emperor Hamayun (1508–56) wanted a magic carpet but settled instead on a tree house. He had a platform built up in a tree, and there he sat to conduct all his business.

Tree advice from Rev. Daniel Stock, minister at Carlisle, Pennsylvania, in 1850–1867: To make a fruit tree bear, "Bore a hole with a half-inch auger into the heart toward sunrise; then put sulphur in and knock a pin on it." For greatest durability of the wood, cut oak and chestnut in the month of August, in the forenoon, and after full moon. Hickory, pine, maple, or other white wood should be cut in the month of August, in the forenoon, and between new moon and the full of the moon.

PEACOCK FEATHERS

Many people like the elegant look of peacock feathers but somehow fear that the "eye" may have something to do with the Evil Eye. In ancient times

the peacock was considered sacred to the goddess Juno, and the "eyes" were
thought to represent the eyes of Argus, her hundred-eyed watchman. When
her husband Jupiter fell in love with Io and changed her into a heifer to
preserve her from his wife's machinations, Juno set Argus to watching the
animal, to prevent her from escaping to be with Jupiter. Hermes, sent by
Jupiter, lulled Argus to sleep, killed him, and freed Io. In memory of her
faithful servant, Juno set his hundred eyes in the tail of her sacred peacock.

Many people use peacock feathers as decorative devices or stand them
upright in vases. One late Victorian householder had a ceiling entirely
covered with their splendor.

Other people will not have the feathers in the house, perhaps believing,
as the ancients did, that where peacock feathers are, no child will be born.
Theater people are notoriously uneasy about them, too, and will not have
them on the stage. The great Shakespearean Sir Henry Irving didn't even
like them in the audience. One night, during the first act of *Othello*, he
noticed a woman in the stalls carrying a feathered accessory. He sent her a
note: "For heaven's sake, take your peacock-feather fan out of the theatre to
save disaster."

CRAZY LIKE A FOX

The cunning of the fox is proverbial and has been for centuries. Though
hunted for sport and as a farmland pest, it has managed to survive by artful
maneuvering rather than speed—by keeping many "earths" into which to
dive, by crossing watercourses to throw foxhounds off the scent, by
backtracking its own trail, by running along fence rails or walls, by taking to
thin ice, by running through a flock of sheep, occasionally by taking refuge in
nearby houses.

Naturally the fox is the subject of many superstitions. Some people
believe that thick fur on foxes in the fall presages a bad winter. Others tell
stories of how foxes sling stolen goose carcasses over their shoulders to carry
them off. Foxes are occasionally believed to rid themselves of fleas by
backing into the water, a leaf held in their mouths, until they are entirely
submerged, so that the fleas must retreat to the leaf or be drowned. For
relief from respiratory ailments, eat a fox's lungs. To see one fox is lucky, but
to see many is unlucky. (Foxes are normally solitary, but mates do stay
together throughout the breeding and kit-rearing season.) The bark of a fox
presages death. To wear a fox's tongue as an amulet cures shyness.

ACORNS

Great superstitions from little acorns grow. The Norsemen associated the oak with Thor, god of storms, who made thunder by flinging his great hammer around the heavens. So they put acorns on their windowsills to protect the house from Thor's anger.

In modern times people put little acorns on the pullstrings of window shades, sometimes encasing real acorns in carefully crocheted jackets, sometimes substituting wooden imitations. Unwittingly they are trying to ward off thunder and lightning.

As for the oak itself, it remains dangerous.

> Beware of the oak.
> It draws the stroke.
> Beware of the ash.
> It courts the flash.
> Creep under the thorn.
> 'Twill protect you from harm.

They say lightning will never strike the elm, or the walnut tree.

FOR THE BIRDS

The bluebird signifies happiness and good luck. The raven croaks of evil. The sparrow kept in a cage in the house will bring bad luck; William Blake said that "puts all Heaven in a rage." A robin flying into your house brings good luck. To kill a dove brings terrible luck, and to rob any bird's nest is to invite disaster. If a bird strikes one of your windowpanes, or if an owl hoots ominously, death may be near for someone in the house. Old superstition has it that a pigeon frequenting your house is good news, but many people very much dislike them nonetheless. When the rooks leave the rookery, expect the worst—worse than rats leaving a sinking ship, in fact.

"WHEN THE WHIPPOORWILL CALLS . . ."

The whippoorwill, because of its dark color and its nocturnal habits, has long been associated with the occult. Moreover, it is often heard just before

dawn, when evil spirits are considered particularly powerful. The spirits are presumably getting in their last licks before they must disappear with the crowing of the cock.

If you hear a whippoorwill near your house, it may be carrying a message of impending death. Even if you cannot see the bird, point your finger in the direction of the sound and "shoot" it. That will counter the evil.

In spring, a young woman who hears the first call of the whippoorwill should listen carefully. One call means the man of her dreams will turn up. Two calls means she will have to wait another year.

Some Amerindians used to say that if you hear two whippoorwills singing together ("hoin, hoin"), you should shout, "No!" If the birds cease at once, the hearer can expect to die shortly, but if they continue to call, the hearer can look forward to a long life. Two whippoorwills are always a bad sign, but fortunately these birds are nearly always solitary.

Never disturb the nests of any birds (bad luck will follow), but be especially careful not to destroy whippoorwill eggs. For each one you destroy, it is said, a member of your family will suffer misfortune.

DOVE OF HAPPINESS

White doves nesting in the beams of one's house are considered good luck by many Islamic peoples. Ali, son-in-law and cousin of Mohammed, used to wish his friends the blessing of white doves. He is reputedly buried in a mosque in Afghanistan, where, it is said, flocks of white pigeons have guarded his tomb for centuries. It is certainly true that if a pigeon with black feathers in its plumage tries to roost there, the white ones drive it violently away.

NESSIE REARS HER UGLY HEAD

Is the famed Loch Ness "monster" fact or fiction, science or superstition? The long, cold, immensely deep Highland lake has been thought for many centuries to be the home of a supernatural "water horse." In recent times, hundreds of people claim to have sighted "Nessie" surfacing, diving, or swimming. Dozens of photographs have been taken, purporting to show a long reptilian neck and a muscular series of "humps" along the creature's back. Divers, exploring the murky depths, occasionally report encountering large moving objects which they cannot identify. Persons of expertise and scientific stature have been sufficiently interested to mount five separate expeditions to explore the loch, equipped with the most modern cameras, recording instruments, and research facilities.

Theories to explain the recorded phenomena range from some sort of giant fish (such as an eel) to a surviving prehistoric marine saurian to masses of decayed vegetation, propelled to the surface and then across it by escaping marsh gas. Nothing has yet been proved, but more and more people are becoming convinced that there'e "something" in Loch Ness.

"ASH GROVE, FAIR ASH GROVE . . ."

My own name, *Ashley*, derives from "ash trees" in a "lea" (field). The ash was revered by the ancient Druids, who worshipped in a sacred grove of ash trees. Think of the charming Welsh folksong "The Ash Grove." Yggdrasil, the great tree of the world in Norse mythology, whose branches extended through the heavens and the earth and the underworld, was an ash tree, and the ash was sacred to many Teutonic peoples. Thus in time there emerged a number of superstitions concerned with the ash.

In ancient rites, people crept through a cleft ash tree, as they did under the dolmen or through the "hole of stone" in the West Country of Britain, to stimulate a kind of new birth and to leave behind disorders and diseases. The ash tree was, as Edmund Spenser wrote, "for nothing ill," so ash was used for the magician's wand (if hazel was not available) and for other magical purposes.

In *Witchcraft and Black Magic*, Montague Summers tells of Cornish children suffering from rupture being "passed through a slit in an ash before sunrise fasting," after which the slit portion was bound together, and this sympathetic magic supposedly caused the rupture to heal. Summers also wrote of country people carrying "a splinter of ash to protect themselves against ill-wish, or as a grand specific for rheumatism." He added:

> The reason for giving ash sap to new-born children in the Highlands of Scotland is, first, because it acts as a powerful astringent, and, secondly, because the ash, in common with the rowan, is supposed to possess the property of resisting the attacks of witches, fairies, and other imps of darkness.

The ash had sinister attributes in the opinion of other peoples. In *The Black Arts*, Richard Cavendish says that "the ash, yew and cypress are associated with death and graveyards," though he also notes that a magic circle is consecrated with "a bunch of vervain, periwinkle, sage, mint, valerian, ash, basil, and rosemary." Ash branches are among the things burned in ritual magic, for even the ashes of ashes are powerful!

Legend has it that the Virgin Mary used ash twigs to make a fire to warm the Christ Child at the Nativity, so ash is often used for cradles, and Anglo-Saxon mothers used to hang the cradles of their children from the branches of the ash trees. If you want your child to grow up to be a good singer, bury its first fingernail parings under an ash tree. Many people in England still believe in that.

WOLVES AND MAN-WOLVES

According to ancient legend, Romulus and Remus, founders of Rome, were suckled by a she-wolf. For many centuries, Romans thought of themselves as Sons of the Wolf, and in other countries legends persist of human children reared by wolves. Such a "wolf-boy" was picked up in Lucknow, India, in 1954, and there have been others. Evidence to prove this, however, is often vague, unreliable, and based on assumption without proof.

The ancients believed it was bad luck just to catch sight of a wolf and that, if he saw you before you saw him, you would lose your voice. If you spoke of a wolf, one would appear—probably with hostile intent. He would not attack a flock of sheep, however, if the shepherd kept a careful count of them. As moderns speak of having a tiger by the tail, Romans said, *Lupum auribus tenere*, "To hold a wolf by the ears."

Belief in werewolves is as old as the Roman Republic and very widespread. Virgil wrote in the Eighth Eclogue, *His ego saepe lapum fieri . . . vidi*, "By means of these [poison plants] I often saw him turned into a wolf. . . ." In France today they speak of the *loup-garou*, in Spain of *lobombre*, in Italy of *lupo mannaro*. In parts of Sicily it is believed that if you can somehow get a wolf's skin to wear, it will give extraordinary courage. In men's minds, the wolf seems to symbolize power.

In Norwegian legend we have the saga of Sigmund the Volsung and his son, Sinfjötli. Adventuring in the forest, they come upon a house in which two men, with great gold rings, are sleeping, and on the wall hang two wolf skins. Sigmund and his son put on the wolf skins as garments and are transformed by their magic into wolves, howling at each other but understanding each other as if they spoke words. They run off into the forest and slay many men. On the tenth day, weary with slaughter, they are back at the house, where they shed the skins and the spell that they had taken over from the two sleeping men, who turn out to be the king's sons, under enchantment. This story obviously has something to do with the wild Vikings who, dressed in furs, went berserk and ravaged the countryside, despoiling, raping, destroying.

OTHER MAN-ANIMALS

In other cultures, men were believed to turn into other animals who represented wildness and strength. In Greece they had a wereboar, in Walachia (Rumania) a weredog, in China a werefox, in other parts of the Orient a weretiger, in Java and Malaya a wereleopard, in Central America a were-eagle and a wereserpent, in Chile a werevulture, and among American Plains Indians a werebuffalo.

DOGS

Dogs, which have lived so close to man for so many eons, have given rise to even more superstitions than wolves. Ghostly dogs protect long-dead people, demon dogs accompany witches, headless dogs run rampant in legend, and even real dogs are involved in superstitions.

In Tibet, people in bad health or out of luck make little human figures out of dough and throw them to the dogs as "ransom"—a cheap and effective way to escape one's troubles. (Tibetans might consider purchasing American "people crackers," canine tidbits in the shape of mailmen and other people frequently attacked by dogs.)

Fernand Mery in *The Life, History and Magic of the Dog* recounts a number of superstitious beliefs about the dog. He says dogs were venerated in ancient Egypt and since then often believed to have a kind of ESP:

> A dog was fast asleep on the terrace of a villa at Antibes when [an eyewitness] saw it suddenly leap up and run howling to the railings. It was called back and quietened, but then it began to behave even more strangely. It crouched under the bed of its master and wailed incessantly. It so happened that at the same moment when the dog was wrenched from sleep on the terrace, its owner was killed in a car accident several miles from Nice.

The loyalty of dogs to their masters is proverbial, of course, the most famous being that of Greyfriars Bobby, a small Scots dog who slept for fourteen years, 1858–1872, summer and winter, on the grave of his master. Not one of the many eminent Scots buried in this Edinburgh churchyard is as famous throughout the world as Bobby.

Superstition caused dogs to be used to pull up mandrake roots. These roots—shaped like a man, our ancestors thought—were believed to have magical powers, but when they were torn from the earth they made a sound so like a human cry that it was thought it would drive a man insane. Therefore, the plant was tied to a dog's tail, and *he* pulled it up, for dogs were believed to be immune.

Dogs were often regarded as the familiar spirits of witches and wizards. They were considered to be emissaries of the Devil in animal form, bestowed upon their earthly masters to do their bidding. In Goethe's *Faust*, Mephistopheles first approaches Doctor Faustus in the form of a dog. Cornelius Agrippa, a sixteenth-century German student of the occult, had a large black dog that followed him everywhere—worked with him, slept with him. People were convinced that the animal was really a demon in disguise.

BANANAS

In recent years American teenagers went through the Mellow Yellow period, when hippies were convinced that smoking banana peel would get you "high." Methods were handed around among subculture groups for preparing the peels for "tripping," and many young people did indeed claim to have taken off on banana skins—either from too little oxygen or too much imagination.

In New Britain, Bismarck Archipelago, banana skins are taken even more seriously. If you thoughtlessly discard a banana skin, a witch can retrieve it, burn it, and thereby cause you to die a painful death.

RUN, RABBIT, RUN

Alexander Severus, Roman emperor from 222 to 235, attributed his lifelong good looks to the fact that at every single meal he ate rabbit. Down the centuries there have been many superstitions connected with this attractive little animal. If a rabbit crosses the road behind you, it is good luck (trouble is behind you), but if one crosses in front of you, it could mean problems. To avoid the problems, cross yourself, or make an X in the road, spit on it, and walk backward over it before continuing on your way.

In countless tales and folk legends, the rabbit symbolizes the common man—forever persecuted, forever cunningly outwitting his betters. Joel Chandler Harris's *Uncle Remus* stories are literary retellings of West African folktales. Beatrix Potter in *Peter Rabbit* and Richard Adam in *Watership Down* have continued the tradition. It's no wonder that one of modern man's most persistent superstitions concerns the importance of carrying a rabbit's foot.

FLOWER TIME

In Europe chrysanthemums are regarded as flowers of death. Never give them as a present. (A variety of chrysanthemum, pyrethrum, contains an ingredient important in insecticides.) In China, however, they are considered the symbol of autumn, and in Japan their resemblance to the sun makes them virtually sacred.

Some people think the first time you visit people, especially for a dinner party, you should bring along white flowers (no other color). Others say one should never bring white flowers into the house.

Don't let florists put fern along with a bouquet, for fern should never be brought into a house. Other people say fern is a protection against witches.

Never pick the earliest flowers in spring, or ivy or Canterbury bells or a single violet or a hyacinth or a white lilac or one lily of the valley or a leaf off a barberry bush or a pansy with the dew still on it.

Lavender, marigolds, snowdrops, and carnations are all lucky, all associated with the Blessed Virgin. Asters are associated with Venus, the cornflower with the goddess Flora, the daisy with Saint Margaret of Antioch, the lily with Eve, and the shamrock, of course, with Saint Patrick; they are all bringers of good fortune, as are primroses (associated with British Prime Minister Benjamin Disraeli) provided you have a pretty big bunch of them and not just a few.

Many flowers have interesting tales connected with them. The hyacinth is supposedly the metamorphosis of a friend of the god Apollo, who was accidentally slain—the red spot is his blood. The thistle saved the Scots from a Viking invasion, it is reported, when a Norseman in the dark stepped on one and let out an involuntary yelp, which roused the Scots to defend themselves. It is now, of course, the national badge of Scotland as the rose is of England.

Crowns of flowering hazel (which will make your wishes come true) and flowering hawthorn (though legend says hawthorn was used for the Crown of Thorns) are especially lucky.

THE GENTLEMAN WHO PAYS THE RENT

The "gentleman" of the above title is the Irishman's pig, for that was the way the Irish tenant farmer used to refer to this useful beast. Cheaply fed and easily reared, he was often a poor farmer's only cash source, so that the money from his sale might well be the family's only means of scraping up the rent money.

Pigs are often treated with great respect in Ireland, and when the Irish began to emigrate to America they took their pigs along. ("As Irish as Paddy's pig," Americans used to say.) Some superstitions about pigs probably went with them:

It is bad to kill a pig when the moon is waning. The flesh may not take salt (and consequently won't cure), and the bacon will shrink in the pan. Pigs are considered good weather predictors. If you see a pig running with a straw in its mouth, rain is coming; if a pig squeals loudly a storm is on the way—pigs "see wind." If a pig runs off, sickness is coming to the family. If you dream of pigs, you will be asked for money. If you have a run of bad luck and wish to break it, pull a pig's tail. And if you own a pig figurine, break it. Even piggy banks are unlucky. Chip yours a little or, better yet, knock one ear off.

Several religions regard the pig as unclean, but this is a canard. The animal is actually much cleaner than a horse or cow, but it does roll in mud to cool itself off, because it does not have sweat glands.

In some languages it is unlucky to refer to the pig directly. The Chinese call him "the long-nosed general." Among the fisherman of northeast Scotland, one does not mention pigs at sea. Just as touching wood can prevent evil on land, so at sea if a pig is mentioned (especially when baiting the lines, which could ruin the catch), one touches iron. "Even in church," it has been reported, "whenever the story of the Gadarene swine was read, the stalwart fisherman would reach for their bootnails and mutter, 'cauld airn' [cold iron]."

Pigs, being more intelligent than dogs, make good familiars for witches and are supposed sometimes to accompany those who have sold their souls to the Devil. If the appropriate charms are used, they will dig up truffles for you. The natives of Sumatra save the jawbones of the pigs they have eaten and suspend them from the ceiling. This is thought to guarantee the salvation of each little porker's soul.

CATS

The Egyptians had a cat god, Bast. She was the goddess of pleasure and protected men against contagious disease and other evils. In Bast's honor, they mummified cats.

The ancient Hebrews believed the ashes of a black kitten would enable one to see demons. Today people are afraid when a black cat crosses their path. In Britain it's unlucky to say the word *cat* while you're down in a mine. In Texas they say you're lucky if a black cat comes into your house, provided it stays. In Lancashire, it's unlucky if a cat dies in your house. It's bad luck for a family to move a cat. Among the Azande of Africa, some women are supposed to give birth to cats; nobody can deny this, for to see one of them is to die. The Chinese emperors slept on cat-shaped pillows for luck.

Buddhists will tell you where cats come from. A rat ate part of one of Buddha's scriptures, so the Enlightened One rubbed a little skin off the inside of his arm and from that made the first cat. The proof? Rats are still afraid of cats.

RATS

Rats are another animal, like foxes, about whom many queer stories are told. They are thought to free one another from traps by gnawing away caught tail tips or by springing the mechanism. Witnesses have reported seeing rats transport a stolen egg to their nest through a cooperative technique: one lies on its back, clinging to the egg, the other pulls its friend across the floor by its tail.

There are many traditional methods of ridding a building of an infestation of rats. In New England, you write the unwanted creatures a letter, telling them that they must leave your premises and suggesting a nearby house where they might be more comfortable. You then grease the paper to make it more palatable to them and push it into the rathole. It is soon digested. So, superstition says, is the message on it.

Rats are perhaps most famous as foretellers of maritime disaster. Rats leaving a sinking ship are a classic symbol of escape from falling fortune. In July 1889, three hands aboard the *Paris C. Brown*, a riverboat plying between Cincinnati, Ohio, and Plaquemine, Louisiana, saw some rats leaving the ship, and in a panic they walked off too. They turned out to be the sole survivors of the *Brown*, for after sailing it was never heard from again. Literally. Not even wreckage of the *Brown* was ever found. The vessel disappeared—completely, permanently, mysteriously.

FISH

St. Malo, the French seaport, still sees fishermen throw back the first fish of the season, for luck. But first they pour a lot of wine down its throat.

The idea is that it will tempt all the other fish to hurry up and get caught so they, too, can get drunk.

Most dreams of fish are said to forecast good luck. The fish is a symbol of life, fishing is a sign of peaceful life, and to see a fish in the water is to receive unexpected favors. A dead fish means loss, and cleaning and dressing a mackerel stands for "deceit and evil tidings."

DRAGON BONES

The belief that many ills can be cured with "dragon bones" in powdered form has cost China a precious, irreplaceable part of its ancient history.

For decades, farmers digging in their fields in Anyang have unearthed certain old bones inscribed with designs that the modern scholar Liu Ngo finally identified as the ancient writing of the Shang people. But before the nature and value of these records could be established by archaeologists, much of this treasure was sold to apothecaries, who pulverized the bones and sold them as "dragon bones."

About 1928, the importance of these finds (and ceremonial vessels of bronze and other artifacts) was established. Well-organized scientific expeditions disinterred treasures from one hundred tombs, ten of them sites of elaborate royal burials. Thus some of the Shang heritage was preserved, but much of China's distant past was lost with the inscriptions on the old "dragon bones."

STORKS

Centuries ago there was already a superstition that a stork flies over a house where a birth is about to take place. It's a small step from that to the legend of the stork as the bringer of babies and of good luck.

So valued are storks as symbols of domestic bliss—for which their habit of mating for life provides a good example—that when these birds began to disappear recently from parts of northeastern Europe, whole regions cooperated in campaigns to induce the birds to return. Pollution controls were instituted, telephone lines raised or lowered so that they would no longer interfere with the birds' flight patterns, and new buildings provided with stork-attracting chimneys. The stork population has begun to rise again, and so have the hopes of their delighted hosts.

EGGS

In Siberia it was believed that shamans (witch doctors) were born from iron eggs laid in larch trees by a large mythical bird.

It's unlucky to use the word *egg* aboard ship.

Eggs are symbolic of life and fertility. Our Easter eggs represent the Resurrection and the renewal of life that comes with spring. In Washington, D.C., they roll them on the White House lawn. In the Ukraine they still decorate them with symbols that recall the ancient days of sun worship.

China's best-known eggs are the so-called hundred-year-old ones, a delicacy. (Actually they have been preserved for considerably less time than that, probably ten years.) Chinese also decorate a baby's layette with designs featuring eggs for good luck. These eggs have eyes to "see" that the child is protected.

A GALLIMAUFRY

The reason a horse blows on water before drinking at night is that water sometimes sleeps, and if an animal were to drink sleeping water, it would die. Blowing wakes the water up.

If you try to kill a snake after dark, it will not die.

Never kill flies toward the end of the year, for you will suffer a $100 loss for each fly killed.

German farmers dread turning up a turnip in the shape of a shriveled hand.

A black lamb means good luck for the flock.

It is bad luck to meet a white horse.

If a rooster crows while facing the door, expect the visit of a stranger.

Leap year, say the Scots, was never a good year for sheep.

Certain mushrooms grow in a circle, called a fairy ring. The Irish believe these rings are caused by the Good People circling in round dances.

3
Medicine and Health

CHARMS AND PREVENTIVES

The common man of yore, who had no access to doctors, knew that his best hope of living for a long time lay in not falling ill. Therefore, innumerable charms were thought up for warding off disease.

Rheumatism. Carry an animal's foot bone (preferably a hare's right forefoot) or an amber charm. Or wear an eelskin around the waist. Or carry in your pocket a potato that has been begged or stolen from someone else. Or carry buckshot in your pocket, or a horse chestnut. Or carry a piece of mountain ash. Or wear a ring made from a silver coffin handle. Or tie a brass wire around your wrist. Or avoid "unclean" habits in youth (advice from the Delaware Indians).

Fits. Carry ash twigs in silk bags. Or go to the parish church at midnight on June 23 (that is, as Midsummer Day is about to break), walk three times up and down each aisle and crawl three times under the Communion table from north to south—this last as the clock is striking twelve. Or grate a small portion of human skull and sprinkle it on the potential sufferer's food. Or collect nine silver coins and nine sets of three halfpennies from nine bachelors (if the sufferer is a woman, from maidens if the sufferer is a man). The silver coins should be made into a ring for the epileptic to wear, and the halfpennies are given to the jeweler or whoever makes the ring.

Colds. Catch an oak leaf before it touches the ground. Or rub yourself with bear grease.

Ague. Tie a red ribbon to someone else's gate. The affliction will then attack him instead of you. Or cut off a lock of hair, wrap it around a pin, and

37

stick it in the bark of an aspen tree; then say, "Aspen tree, aspen tree, I pray thee shake instead of me."

Tuberculosis. Smear yourself with dog's fat. Or swallow baby frogs before breakfast.

Toothache. Carry a double nut in your pocket. Or wear around your neck in a little bag a tooth taken from a corpse. Or do the same with the forelegs and one hind leg from a mole. Or put on stockings or trousers right leg first.

For all-around good health, wear around your neck a pebble exposed for three nights to the beams of the moon. Or wear a stone with a natural hole in it—a powerful charm, especially against witchcraft and fairies.

WARTS

There are almost too many cures for warts to count. Many of them work, too, for warts often disappear spontaneously, no matter what you do. Here are some things superstition recommends for warts.

Steal a dishrag and hide it in a stump. Or rub the warts with "stones, peas, beans, or seeds" and then throw the latter away. Or tie as many knots in a string as you have warts and bury the string; as the string rots, the warts will disappear. Or put vinegar on your wart and on a penny at the same time; as the copper corrodes, your wart will vanish.

Rub a wart with corn, then bore a hole in a tree, insert the corn, and plug up the hole. Or fill your mouth with corn, dig a hole, spit the corn into the hole, and cover it up. Or rub the wart with a sassafras leaf or soda bread or a piece of onion (then throw it away). Or rub the wart with a penny.

Capture a large black snail, rub it over your warts, then hang it up on a thorn; do this nine nights in succession. Or rub your wart with raw meat (preferably stolen), wrap the meat in paper, and throw it away in a spot where a dog will find it.

Cut a notch in a stick for each wart and burn the twig. Or say your prayers backward over the wart. Or take a nail you have touched to the wart and make a cross with it on a pecan tree. Or wash your warts in water in which eggs have been boiled. Or put a drop of blood from the wart into a hollowed-out kernel of corn and throw the kernel to the chickens.

Or kill a cat and bury it in a black stocking. Or steal a piece of steak and bury it where three roads meet. Or bury a rooster's comb. Or rub the wart with a peeled apple and then give the apple to a pig.

When a funeral is passing, rub your warts and say, "May these warts and this corpse pass away and nevermore return."

SALIVA

From very ancient times human saliva was thought to have the power to cure wounds, to ward off evil, to attract good luck. Dancers spit into their ballet shoes, workmen spit on their hands before launching into a job, actors spit on either side of you to bring you luck. Fighters spit on their hands for luck.

Christ used His saliva to heal the sick, to bring back sight to the blind.

Businessmen spit on the *Handsel*, the first money taken for the day. (To be lucky, the *Handsel* must be "well wet.") A successful bettor spits on his winnings.

Spittle is an ingredient in many charms. It was mixed with dirt and oil and smeared on foreheads. It was spat into water in which two persons had (presumably inadvertently) washed. It was used to moisten dry ingredients in poultices and doses, somehow conveying to them the power of life.

Spitting to change bad luck to good is almost a worldwide practice. Some Australian aborigines spit whenever a dead man's name is mentioned. Ancient Greeks spat three times at the sight of an epileptic or madman. Old women in Greece and Rome would spit three times to ward off the Evil Eye, especially if it was thought to be threatening a child. English rustics spat three times if they saw a piebald horse, a dead dog, or a person lame in the right leg.

METALS AS MEDICINE

Certain metallic elements were thought to contain important magic properties and to ward off or cure illness.

Iron was hated by fairies and witches, who would not approach it. (It was suspected that these supernatural creatures were, in fact, survivors of Bronze Age people, inimical to newcomers who possessed iron tools and weapons.) To preserve the family from spells and prevent fairies from carrying off newborn children, a piece of iron was laid on the threshold or a horseshoe tacked up over the door. When something evil or dangerous was mentioned, men touched iron (as moderns knock on wood). To prevent disease, men wore iron rings or amulets.

But it was considered bad luck to bring old iron into the house. No plant with magical virtues should be cut with iron. In some parts of Europe it was considered bad luck to plow with iron-tipped plowshares, and many buildings, especially sacred ones, were erected without the use of iron nails.

Gold and silver were associated with the sun and the moon respectively, often male and female as well. Gold ruled the heart and was prescribed by early physicians—for wealthy patients, it need hardly be said—as a tonic and a cordial, a strengthener of the heart. Silver ruled the head and was prescribed for melancholia, failure of memory, and epilepsy.

Antimony, mercury, lead, sulfur, tin, bismuth, zinc—all these had passing phases as medicines. Today the chief mineral prescribed for health and human diet is iron. No wonder fairies are seen no more.

SNEEZING

Gesundheit means "health," and it's what Germans (and many others) say when people sneeze. Why? Because of an old superstition that when a person sneezes his soul for an instant flies out of his body. A quick blessing will prevent the entry of a demon at this awkward time.

Some people like to sneeze. Truman Capote claims that seven sneezes in a row are as good as an orgasm. (Not everyone agrees with him.)

Sneezes were often signs of good things. If a sailor sneezed on the starboard side of a vessel as it embarked, it would have a lucky voyage. If he sneezed on the port side, it would encounter foul weather. If you sneeze in the morning before breakfast, you will receive a present before the week is out. If you sneeze before you get up on Sunday, it means that a wedding is approaching. If a sick person sneezes, he will recover. Sneezing three times in a row is a sign of good luck.

But it's bad luck for a bride or groom to sneeze during the wedding ceremony.

The Scots believed that a newborn baby was under a fairy's spell until it gave its first sneeze; then the spell was broken. Scots midwives often carried snuff with them to induce sneezing.

A once familiar rhyme summarizes the meaning of sneezes:

Sneeze on Monday, sneeze for danger;
Sneeze on Tuesday, kiss a stranger;
Sneeze on Wednesday, get a letter;
Sneeze on Thursday, something better;
Sneeze on a Friday, sneeze for sorrow;
Sneeze on Saturday, see your sweetheart tomorrow.
Sneeze on Sunday, your safety seek,
Or the Devil will have you all the week.

The Zulus believe that a sneeze summons *makosi* (spirits). The natives of Calabar say, "Far from you!" and make a gesture of shooing away evil. Some Christians cross themselves. Some say, "Bless me!" The Samoans say, "Life to you."

Sir Thomas Browne, writing of superstitions, mentioned the belief that when the king of Monomotapa sneezed, blessings were broadcast all over the sky.

Garcilaso de la Vega, Peruvian historian, records that when the native chief Guachoya sneezed, all his courtiers cried, "Save you!" prompting the great explorer Hernando de Soto to remark, "Do you not see all the world is one?"

In fact, all the world does seem to be "one" on some of these remarkably universal superstitions.

BURNS

A wide variety of folk remedies are advocated for treatment of burns. American Indians used honey, an infusion of pine bark, or wilted Jimson-weed leaves (applied externally, of course, for Jimson weed is a deadly poison if ingested).

A poultice of mashed potatoes is an American remedy (and possibly a useful one, for the puree must seal off the injury from infection and keep it moist while healing).

Goose dung mixed with the bark of the elder tree was an English cure for burns, as was touching the burn with some item of church linen such as an altar cloth or chalice napkin. But in Great Britain people relied mainly on charms for healing burns.

Lay your hand over the burned spot, blow on it three times, each time saying, "Old clod beneath the clay, burn away, burn away. In the name of God, be thou healed." That's an Irish charm.

In the Shetland Islands, one says:

> Here come I to cure a burnt sore;
> If the dead knew what the living endure,
> The burnt sore would burn no more.

And in the West of England:

> Three Angels came, from North, East and West,
> One brought fire, another brought frost,
> And the third brought the Holy Ghost.
> So out fire and in frost,
> In the Name of the Father, Son, and Holy Ghost.

ITCHING

The presistent torment of itching has driven many people to attempt either to cure it or explain it. Hence the following folk beliefs:

An itchy right palm means money is coming, and an itchy left that money is slipping away. You can break the spell of the latter, however, by rubbing the offending left hand on wood. An itchy right hand can also mean a friend is coming, that you will soon be shaking hands with a stranger, or that you will be having company. If the thumb pricks, however, it portends evil. "By the pricking of my thumbs," says the second witch in *Macbeth*, "something wicked this way comes."

If your nose itches, you will shortly meet a fool and be injured by him. If your right ear itches, someone has said something nice about you; if it's your left, someone has said something not so nice about you. If your right eye itches, you are shortly going to laugh; if it's your left, you are shortly going to cry. If your upper lip itches, you will be kissed by someone tall; if it's your lower, by someone short.

If your knee itches, you will soon be kneeling in a strange church. If your foot itches, you will soon be treading strange ground. If your elbow itches, you will soon be sleeping with a strange bedfellow.

CURES

If, even after all the precautions you have taken, you still manage to fall ill, there are still some measures to be taken. Here are a few folk remedies:

Cramp. Wear an eelskin around the leg to relieve leg cramps. Or wear a moleskin around your left leg. Or tie a cotton string around your ankle. Or lay your shoes across the aching member. Or use cork; wear cork garters or lay pieces of cork between the sheet and the mattress of your bed. Or stand on the leg that has cramp and recite the following:

> Foot, foot, foot is fast asleep;
> Thumb, thumb, thumb, in spittle we steep;
> Crosses three we make to ease us;
> Two for the thieves and one for Jesus.

Best of all for cramp was a cramp ring, usually made from the nails, hinges, or handles of a coffin or—in the American West—from a bent horseshoe nail. Edward the Confessor had a cramp ring, supposedly an aid to stomach cramps; it was handed down for several generations of kings before being lost. Tudor kings revived the fashion, consecrating pieces of silver and gold each Good Friday, which metal was then made into rings. The custom was abandoned by Edward VI.

Rheumatism. Have the patient treated by a woman who has given birth to a child by "footling presentation" (that is, feet first). Or rub pepper into the finger- and toenails (a Javanese cure). Or crawl under bramble bushes, thus "scraping off" the ailment. Or bury the patient up to the neck in a churchyard (old version) or give him a hot mud bath (modern version). Or chew a thistle. Or carry a haddock bone (the haddock has long been considered a "sacred" fish because of the two dark marks just behind its head, said to be the fingermarks of Saint Peter). Or induce bees to sting the affected area—a remedy recently rediscovered under respectable auspices, for bee venom is now thought to counteract the pain of this condition.

Fever. Drink gin, flavored with powdered mole, for nine consecutive mornings. Or chew a turnip. Or place an agate stone on the forehead. Or eat watermelon. Or imbed the fingernail parings of the patient in a ball of wax and stick the wax on a neighbor's door, thus "transferring" the fever to him. Or make three knots in a thread, rub the sufferer with the knots, then throw part of the thread with two of the knots into the fire, saying, "I put the sickness on top of the fire," and tie the rest of the thread with the third knot around the patient's neck.

Toothache. Apply the boiled root pulp of the sumac tree. Or drive a nail into an oak tree (especially one struck by lightning). Or bite off at ground level the first fern that appears in the spring. Or catch a frog, spit into its mouth, and then throw it away. Or apply gunpowder and brimstone. Or apply a splinter from a gallows on which a murderer has been hanged. Or drink water from a human skull. Or touch your mouth with the finger of a dead child. Or take clay from the grave of a priest and say a Paternoster ("Our Father") and an Ave ("Hail, Mary").

Stomach disorders. Tie a cormorant skin to the stomach. Drink an infusion of pine bark.

Headache. Bind the head of a buzzard or the cast-off skin of a snake around the forehead. Or clutch some scraped radish pulp. Or find some moss grown on a human skull, dry it to powder, and use it like snuff. Or nail a lock of the sufferer's hair to a tree, preferably aspen or ash. Or wear a rope noose with which a man has been hanged.

Bleeding. Apply cobweb. Or (for nosebleed) push a cold key down the back or hold a table knife to the upper lip. Or wear a dead toad in a bag around the neck or a lace from the shoe of a member of the opposite sex. In fairness to folk beliefs, however, it ought to be pointed out that ordinary people at least tried to stanch bleeding; their "betters," the learned doctors who attended the rich and important, often deliberately caused bleeding in the belief that it relieved fever and released the demons of disease, the humours.

Epilepsy. Every two hours, take a concoction of pulverized horse hock. Or wear a ring made from a half-crown donated to a church collection. Or take the victim's nail parings and a lock of his hair and bury them together with a live cock at the spot where the victim fell down in his last seizure. Or drink an infusion of mistletoe. Or wear a necklace made from nine pieces of elder wood. Or eat the heart of a black jackass on toast. Or drive a nail into the ground at the spot where the epileptic fell. Or for nine days in a row eat the heart of a crow beaten up with its blood.

Boils. Place a poultice over the boils for three days and nights; then place the poultices with their cloths in the coffin of somebody about to be buried. Or hang three nutmegs or a camphor bag around the neck. Or induce a friend to go to a cemetery for you and walk six times around the grave of a recently interred corpse. Or steep the petals of the madonna lily in brandy, then apply to the boil, rough side down.

Injuries or sores. Keep the instrument or weapon bright until the wound heals. Cut a slit in the stomach of a freshly killed animal and thrust the sore member into it; as the stomach cools down, the sores will heal. Or sleep on a bearskin.

Colds. Boil sumac leaves in beer and drink the brew. Or stuff a thin slice of orange rind up each nostril. Or eat dried rats' tails.

Erysipelas. This streptococcal infection, highly contagious, is characterized by high fever and outbreaks of rough, reddened areas on the skin. It used to be much more common than it is today, and hence there were a number of spells for curing it. Apply sheep's dung as a poultice to the eruptions. Or strike sparks from stone and steel in such a way that they will touch the face. Or cut off one ear of a cat—or its tail—and allow the blood to drip on the affected part. Or wear a piece of elder wood around the neck; it must be a piece cut between two knots on which the sun has never shone. Or pass a red-hot poker near the face three times, chanting:

> Three holy men went out walking;
> They did bless the heat and the burning;
> They blessed it that it might not increase;
> They blessed it that it might quickly cease;
> And guard against inflammation and mortification,
> In the Name of the Father, the Son, and the Holy Ghost.

Miscellaneous cures. For earache: blow tobacco smoke in the ear or prick a snail and apply a drop of the moisture that comes out. For gout: take hairs from the affected leg, plus the sufferer's nail parings, put them into a hole made in an oak, and seal it with cow dung. For jaundice: eat nine lice on a piece of bread and butter. For wens: touch a dead man's hand. For baldness: drink sage tea or anoint the bald spot with goose dung. For drunkenness: put a live eel or the eggs of an owl in the drunken man's drink. (To prevent herself from marrying a drunkard, a girl should make sure she never gets wet when doing the laundry.) For colic: stand on your head for fifteen minutes or jump through a midsummer bonfire, or drink wolf dung mixed with white wine. For sore eyes: apply tea or rainwater that fell on Holy Thursday or an ointment made of salt, human milk, and crushed bed bugs. For scarlet fever: cut some hair from the patient's head and stuff it down the throat of a donkey. For frostbite: apply a poultice of cow manure and milk. For goiter: take a common snake by head and tail and draw it nine times across the swelling; then put the snake, alive, in a bottle.

General sickness. Wash the patient and throw the water over the cat. Or make a chalk mark on an iron kettle and put it on the fire; as the mark burns off, the disease will be driven out. In Tibet, if a doctor happens to be out of the precise remedy you require, he writes your prescription on a piece of paper; then you take the prescription—literally. You swallow the piece of paper, for it's considered the same as taking the medicine itself.

HANDS

The hand, along with upright posture, imagination, reasoning ability, and fear of the future, is one of the marks that distinguish man from animals. It is not surprising that the hand is involved in many superstitious beliefs.

A moist hand is supposed to be the sign of an amorous nature. Cold hands are a sign of a warm heart. If two people wash hands in the same basin at the same time, they will soon quarrel and part. It is lucky to have a left-handed pitcher in baseball. If a baby's hands are washed before it's a year old, he will never have money. Shake hands with the right, and you'll have good luck; with the left, bad luck. If four people shake hands with the pairs crossed, a wedding is in the offing. But if the hands of two people cross while reaching for something, look for a quarrel between them. A hand must cover the mouth when you are yawning, or the Devil may enter through it.

The Romans had names for the four fingers, indicating their uses: index finger, *salutaris* (healthy, useful); middle finger, *medius* (middle), but also *impudicus* and *infamis* (shameless, disgraceful) because indecent gestures were performed with it; ring finger, *anularis* (ring); and little finger, *parvus* (little). Images of hands were frequently used as amulets, usually to signify power. To ward off the Evil Eye, of course, one made signs with one's hands.

The laying on of hands was regarded as a most potent gesture of healing, particularly if the person who did the laying on was powerful or holy. The touch of kings was considered especially efficacious. The royal touch for curing diseases probably got its start with Louis IX (1215–70), crusader and lawgiver, canonized as Saint Louis by Boniface VIII in 1297. This pious king of France was credited with miracles even while he was alive, and he cured many of scrofula, tuberculosis of the lymph glands, by the touch of his hand.

French and English royal families frequently intermarried, so the blood of Saint Louis ran in the veins of the English kings as well. Therefore English kings also used to "touch for the scrofula," or "king's evil." After they more or less gave it up, the eighteenth-century earl of Chesterfield took it up for a while, until the embarrassment of his friends called a halt.

Today many still believe in the efficacy of touching in faith healing. You can see it in many churches and at revival meetings and "crusades" and even on televised religious shows. Many cures are claimed.

The laying on of hands survives in the father's blessing, in the ritual by which a bishop ordains a priest, even in a sense in the friendly touch that demonstrates caring, affection, sympathy.

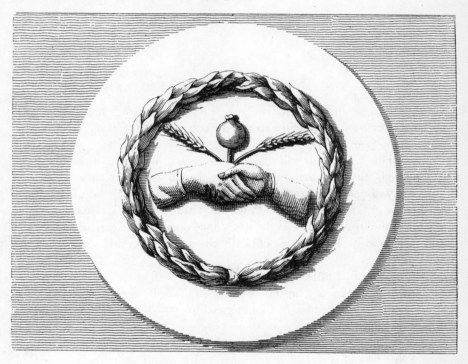

4

Places

WELLS

Many superstitions and religious beliefs are associated with wells, perhaps because water carries strong connotations of life-giving and rebirth to so many people.

Drinking well water will make you grow tall, many Americans believe. In Cornwall, they say that a child baptised with water from the well of St. Ludgvan will never be hanged. If you go to Gulval Well in the same county on the eve of the feast of Saints Peter and Paul (June 28) and ask the water, "Water, water, tell me truly, Is the man I love duly, On the earth or under the sod, Sick or well—in the name of God?" the water will bubble and boil if the news is good.

If a cross of palm fronds is tossed into the well at Little Conan (also in Cornwall) and it floats, the one who throws it will live out the year. The Silver Well at Llanblethian in Glamorganshire was the place for sweethearts to test one another out. A blackthorn twig was thrown into the water; if it floated, the lover was faithful, and if it sank, he was not. If it whirled around, your lover was cheerful; if it stayed put, he would be sullen.

At Altarnum (Cornwall), lunatics were dunked in the waters of St. Nun's Well and tossed until the frenzy left them. St. Tecla's Well water cured epilepsy. So did that of St. Fegla's Well, Caernarvonshire. Eglys Well in Lleyn, Wales, granted wishes; but first you had to descend the steps to the well, fill your mouth with water, walk up again, and walk around the church without spilling a drop. St. Servan's Well was good for the eyes and the toothache, but after washing in the water, the patient had to sleep all night in the chapel. At St. Madron's Well, near Penzance, shingles, wild fire, and other skin complaints were cured by a dunking; afterward, the patient (usually a child) was carried nine times around the spring and then a piece of his garment was left behind.

At the Llanbedrog Well in Lleyn, you could learn the name of a thief. You threw a piece of bread into the water and then named the persons you suspected. When you came to the right name, the bread would sink.

Britain has a number of "granny" wells dedicated to Saint Anne, grandmother of Jesus, as well as wells dedicated to such local saints as those mentioned above. Pious people still deck these wells with garlands on certain festive days.

In Derbyshire, wells are often decorated with streamers, farm produce, flower petals pressed into wet clay, and such. About June 25 each year, parishioners at Brislington process to the ruins of St. Anne's Well. Around Ascension Day, wells are dressed at Tissington; in June at Wicksworth, Ashford-in-the-Water, Youlgrave, Tideswell, and Hope; in July at Buxton and Marsh Lane; in August at Bonsall, Stoney Middletown, Bradwell, Barlow, Eyam, and Wormhill.

OUTCROPS AND WONDER ROCKS

There's magic and myth in stones—especially large, oddly shaped, or out-of-place boulders (such as those carried by glaciers many miles from where they were picked up). Here are the tales told of some of these formations.

Perhaps the best-known geologic formation in the world is the Giant's Causeway, near Bushmills in Antrim, Northern Ireland. It is a mass of hexagonal basaltic columns standing bolt upright, ground level to forty feet in height. Some parts of it extend seven hundred feet out to sea, hence the name "Causeway." The Irish say that once, long ago, the giants built a bridge from Ireland to Scotland, and that this is what remains of it.

At Shebbear in Devonshire, every November 5 (Guy Fawkes' Day), people make a public ceremony of turning over a large stone that lies under an ancient oak. This is said to prevent bad luck during the following year, for the stone is supposed to have been dropped into the village square by the Devil himself.

Starved Rock on the Illinois River, near Ottawa, Illinois, is a high, isolated, free-standing mesa. According to legend, it was here in the 1680s that a remnant of the Illinois Indians took refuge from the marauding Iroquois and held them off until food supplies ran out.

East of Edinburgh and within sight of Holyrood Palace is an eight-hundred-foot hill known as Arthur's Seat. Tradition says that it was from this elevated spot that King Arthur surveyed the surrounding region and watched his knights defeat the Saxons in a great battle.

In the sandy southern regions of Australia's Northern Territory, an astonishing outcrop of rust-colored rock juts up 1,143 feet above the plain. Ayers Rock is regarded by the aborigines of the continent as the home of their original ancestors, and the lair of hare-wallaby men, poison-snake people, and other denizens from their tribal legends.

In southwestern Arizona are located the aptly named Superstition Mountains, the site, if so immense an area can be called a site, of the famed Lost Dutchman mine. This fabled gold strike, reputedly the richest in the world, has been found and lost, found and lost so many times that prospectors believe it to be cursed. No one, having once located it and left it to get help in working the claim (the belief goes) has ever been able to find it again.

GARDENS

Garden lore, like that for farming, depends heavily on folk beliefs. Here are a few common ones.

Planting. Above-ground crops should be sown as the moon is on the wane; root crops, such as turnips, potatoes, carrots, etc., should be planted when the moon is waxing. Algonquian Indians planted corn when the leaves of the tree were the size of the mouse's ear. English farmers tested the temperature before sowing grain by pulling down their pants and sitting on the ground; if the soil was not too cold for them, it was not too cold for the barley. Some recommend that turnips and rampion be planted by a naked man. But, in any event, never sow the last three days of March—unlucky—and beans must be planted before May. And sow thickly:

> One for the rook, one for the crow;
> One to die, and one to grow.

Good friends and bad friends. Foxglove and camomile are said to be helpful and sustaining to other plants that grow nearby, whereas ash trees are bad for some neighboring plants, and walnuts must not be allowed to sprout near tomatoes or they will spoil the flavor.

Here are some things you can expect from your vegetable patch.

Beans. Accidents and the onset of lunacy are more common when the broad bean is in flower. However some people believe that the flowers of this plant smell so sweet that they must contain the souls of dead men. When eaten, they give you bad dreams.

Parsley. This is an unlucky plant. The ancient Greeks regarded it as a symbol of mourning, and it was most unfortunate to encounter a growing patch of it while you were marching to war. In England, there were taboos against cutting it, transplanting it, giving it away, and even growing it at all.

Asparagus. The wild variety was used in ancient Greece for wedding garlands, so it is regarded as a lucky plant. Always leave one stem uncut and allow it to blossom.

Cabbage. If it grows double—two shoots from one root—it is very lucky, as are cabbages that grow with widely opened leaves. A leaf tied around the throat is a cure for sore throat, and the juice (mixed with honey) eases hoarseness and laryngitis. In parts of France and Belgium it is believed that newborn infants are grown in the cabbage patch—boys in white cabbages, girls in red. (At least that's what children are told. One little French girl the author has heard of, learning that a new baby was on the way, went out and cut down all the red cabbages. She wanted a baby brother.)

Lettuce. Some people regard lettuce as a kind of contraceptive—an excess of it in one's garden, and the woman of the house will not conceive. On the other hand, Juno is thought to have conceived Hebe after eating lettuce, so it seems to work both ways.

Peas. A peapod containing only one pea is lucky. One with nine peas must be thrown over the shoulder while you make a wish, which will then come true.

Carrot. This can be an ingredient in love potions.

Endive. Even if you don't like this vegetable in salad, plant it as a kind of clock. Its leaves open at eight in the morning, it is said, and close at four—an eight-hour day.

Cress. Eating this will make you witty.

Onion. This vegetable is regarded as an aid to deafness and good in a sickroom. To dream of eating onions means that you will have much domestic strife.

Potato. Plant these roots with the eyes up, so that they can see to grow.

When you dig the first potatoes of the season, all the family must partake of them, or the rest of the potatoes will not keep.

Cucumber. In addition to its reputation for coolness, still with us today, cucumber was considered an aid to love affairs and a cure for rabies.

Strawberry. This is one of many plants of which the Virgin is said to be particularly fond. Fairies and elves like the fruit also, and in Bavaria farmers used to tie the leaves to the horns of their cattle to protect them from spells.

Here are some things to expect from your herb garden.

Rosemary. This herb is a great comforter to the heart and, if worn about the person, an aid to memory.

Sage. This plant was considered to be good for virtually everything: the liver, the blood, the brain, the muscles, the stomach, the heart, and the nerves. "Why should a man die whilst sage grows in his garden?" ran a medieval saying. But if, in spite of everything, a sage-eating man died, it was considered sage to plant sage on his grave.

Centaury. Anxiety will not bother the person who eats centaury, and if a girl washes her face in a decoction of the plant, it will take away freckles.

Vervain. This herb will cure grief, can be used in a love potion, and (if the latter is successful) makes an excellent bridal wreath.

Bay. The leaves purge a man of choler and phlegm. If thrown on the fire and found to crackle, that's a good sign; if they burn silently, you will have bad luck. Placed under pillows, they give sweet dreams. Or wrap a bay leaf around a wolf's tooth and put it under the pillow, and your dreams will tell you where your stolen money has been hidden.

Rue. Make a disinfectant from this herb. Plant it next to sage to help that useful herb to thrive. Some Turks consider rue a good luck symbol. (Edie Gormé, who is part Turkish, is said to carry a growing rue plant with her on tour.)

Borage. Mixed with hellebore, this plant will "purge the veins of melancholy, and cheer the heart of those black fumes which make it smart." It is also supposed to heal abscesses. Incidentally, it produces a tall handsome plant with exquisite blue flowers.

Bugloss. This herb is good for "harmful wicked moistness of the lung," for coughs, and for swollen feet. When mixed with hot water it "maketh a man to have a good mind."

Pennyroyal. This variety of mint is supposed to cure nausea, "cold humor in the head," boils, and cramp.

Briony. Considered a "martial" plant, briony was often an ingredient in witches' spells (the berries contain a dangerous poison), but the tender young sprouts could be pickled safely and the roots made a useful cathartic.

MINES

People who descend into the bowels of the earth every day and earn a hard living in semidarkness can hardly help but develop folk beliefs of many sorts. The oldest perhaps is their belief in small supernatural creatures who work near them underground but can seldom be seen.

The Cornish tin miners believe in the Knockers, diminutive creatures in miners' leather clothes who can be heard working away with their picks in nearby galleries. By following the sounds of these knocks, men can locate the richest veins of ore. Sometimes the Knockers also warn miners of impending cave-ins or other disasters. However, one must never mark a cross underground, for the Knockers are enemies of Christianity and will resent it.

In Germany dwarfs are believed to live underground, mining and storing up treasures of gold, silver, and (especially) gems of all kinds. (The seven little men in "Snow White" were miners of this sort.) Do a kindness for one of these creatures, and he will reward you with what looks like a heap of coals, but when you get the heap home it will turn out to be a collection of jewels.

More prosaic beliefs of those who work in the mines are concerned with good luck and bad luck, like those of their neighbors above ground. To meet a woman on the way to the pit or a cross-eyed person or a rabbit (especially if you are on the night shift) is very bad luck. The same goes for seeing a snail, although one can drop a bit of tallow from one's candle and thus ward off that evil. It is bad luck to return to one's house after setting out for work. Superstitious miners, having forgotten their packed lunches, often work without food all day rather than go back to fetch them. A dove or robin flying around the pithead foretells disaster; many miners will not go to work if they see that. A dream of broken shoes is also bad luck. Washing his back will bring a miner trouble, possibly cause a cave-in.

IRELAND

Many places in Ireland are "magical" sites, often of pre-Christian origin. At Arboe, County Tyrone, there are both a Christian cross and a pagan wishing tree, the latter studded with nails driven in by believers. At Armagh, site of the primate since Patrick's time and earlier a center of pagan witchcraft, a museum contains items of folkloric interest, some documenting early superstitions which have not entirely died out in Ireland even to this day.

Lough Larne in Northern Ireland is said to be the site of a ferry inaugurated by Saint Patrick himself. In fifteen hundred years, no drowning has ever been recorded there.

On Slemish Mountain, Antrim, Patrick was a swineherd slave and worked his boyhood miracles. On Mount Cuilcagh, Fermanagh, is a rock throne used from time immemorial for investing the chiefs of the Maguires. At the Giant's Causeway, where early settlers believed the prehistoric giants had been at work, there is a famous wishing seat.

Near Downpatrick, there is a "tomb" of Saint Patrick, though he is not actually buried there. Downpatrick also contains some pre-Christian holy wells.

Derry ("grove of oaks") was probably the site of Druidic practices. The Seven Mountains of Mourne were left by Patrick, they say, as perpetual guardians of Ireland.

On Rathlin Island, seven miles off the coast of Antrim, Robert the Bruce is said to have watched a spider in a cave try over and over again to construct a web. The arachnid's persistence impressed and inspired Bruce, and he found the courage to return to Scotland and renew his war for his country's independence.

The Cloughmore, or large stone, near Rostrevor is said to have been put there by Finn MacCool, the legendary giant. The hole in it became filled with water, and thus Carlingford Lough was created.

And, of course, most famous of all is the Blarney Stone, which is found in the ruins of Blarney Castle (built 1446) in County Cork. Anyone who wants to acquire sophistication, charm, and eloquence can do so by kissing the stone, but he must hang upside down to do it. There's also a fairy glen nearby.

TOMBS AND GRAVES

Concern for the welfare of the dead in the afterworld dates from the very earliest periods that man has occupied the earth. The vast bulk of what we know today about prehistoric peoples has been learned from the artifacts and human remains uncovered from interment sites. Many customs, from very ancient times, have survived in some form to the present day.

To have a stillborn infant buried in the coffin with you is a sure ticket to heaven, many people believe. Place a coin in the coffin so that the deceased can pay his fare across the River Jordan (an obvious survival of the ancient Greek belief in Charon and the River Styx). Bury a woman all in black, and she will return to haunt her family.

The corpse must be taken from the house feet first; if it is able to look back at the family, it may beckon someone else to follow. On the way to the burying ground, the coffin must be carried with the sun behind it, even if this means taking the long way around. The grave itself should be dug on an east-west axis, so that the deceased will face east—toward Gabriel when he blows his horn for the resurrection. The grave should also lie on the south side of the church. Rain falling on the coffin or a clap of thunder at the conclusion of the obsequies means that the deceased has reached heaven.

The first person buried in a newly dedicated cemetery is claimed by the Devil. Never plow up land that was once a burying ground, no matter how long ago. To annoy the dead, urinate on their graves. To raise them, sprinkle the tomb with blood and call them by name.

Troubled by a vampire? Find out where it "lives"—a white horse can lead you there. Dig it up (by daylight) and drive a stake through its heart. Or decapitate it. Or both. Or pour boiling water (to which some vinegar has been added, perhaps a parody of offering wine to the dead) over the grave.

Just as some reliquaries of Christian saints are supplied with openings, so that the faithful can reach in and touch the relics, so in Islam some tombs of holy men are left open at the top so that prayers may reach them. In the Sahara, the dead man's belongings are left at his gravesite: a plate and pitcher, perhaps an ostrich egg. An American Indian's property is so intricately bound up with his person that, unless he specifically wills an item to a relative, all his possessions are burned at his death.

The tomb figurines from Chinese burials represent servants provided for the dead. In some cultures figurines came to be used in place of actual persons sacrificed at the burial of VIPs. In Egyptian tombs, *ushabti* figurines in the form of mummies were provided to be agricultural laborers in the other world.

The strangest death figurines may be the *mulongo* ("double") venerated by African natives. In Britain's Horniman Museum there is a bark-cloth case from the Baganda tribe containing the umbilical cord of a prince, "supposed to retain the ghost of the afterbirth, which was the prince's double."

THE SEA

The lonely sea—the barren sea, as the ancient Greeks called it—kept men from their homes for many months, even years, at a stretch, endangered their lives, often crippled them or caused them to die of scurvy or other diseases, and yet it never lacked for men to sail it. They concentrated their natural anxieties in numerous superstitions.

In ancient times men would not launch a ship, especially a man-of-war, without first blooding its keel. Slaves or prisoners of war were strapped down to the ways, and as the vessel slipped down them to the sea, it crushed the sacrifices. Today, we christen a ship with a bottle of champagne or other wine instead, which both bloods the keel and represents a libation to the gods of the sea.

It is bad luck to sail on a Friday, the first Monday in April, the second Monday in August, and December 31. Friday commemorates the Crucifixion, of course, and the other three are supposed to be anniversaries of the slaying of Abel, the destruction of Sodom and Gomorrah, and the suicide of Judas.

> Sunday sail, never fail.
> Friday sail, ill luck and gale.

If, on your way to the dock, you encounter a barefoot woman or one in a white apron, turn back. The voyage would be unlucky. The same belief holds if you find your earthenware basin turned upside down or if a hawk, owl, or crow alights in the rigging. (But bees and small birds are welcome.)

Once aboard, superstitions thicken. You must not bring an umbrella with you. You must not lend any of the equipment of your ship to another without damaging it slightly. Otherwise all your luck will go out of your ship with it. You must not lose a bucket or mop overboard. You must not mend a flag on the quarterdeck or hand one to another sailor through the rungs of a ladder. During a voyage, you must not wear the clothes of a sailor who has died at sea, or you will follow him overboard. (But once back ashore, they can be worn with impunity.) You must not carry your seaboots over your shoulder, only under the arm. You must not carry flowers aboard ship. If you do they are destined to become a wreath either for a shipmate or for the entire vessel (a superstition particularly strong among submariners). Your friends and family must not watch your ship out of sight, or it will never be seen again. Never stick a knife into a deck.

Beware of Jonahs (ships' jinxes). Among fishermen, a small catch following the signing on of a new hand means that he's a Jonah. Or if a man comes aboard carrying a black valise, that's a jinx. Jonahs bring bad luck to an entire vessel.

So do women and clergymen. The sight of a woman angers the sea— unless she is naked, in which case she can cause gales to subside. (This is supposedly one reason why so many figureheads were images of bare-breasted women.) The clergy were disliked because of their association with death and burials. Even worse was a corpse; a ship cannot make headway with a dead man aboard.

Above all, never change a ship's name. A deadly curse will follow the ill-fated vessel if you do.

To counter all this bad luck, carry the caul of a newborn infant or a feather from a wren killed on New Year's Day (a potent charm against mermaids and sirens). Nail a horseshoe to the mast. Pierce your ears! That is supposed to improve eyesight. Toss a piece of silver at the foot of the mast; better yet, if possible, see that the mast, when stepped, rests on a silver coin.

Sighting a phantom ship such as the *Flying Dutchman* is supposed to mean death or at least blindness for the one who sees it. (However, on July 11, 1881, sixteen-year-old Prince George of England, then a young naval cadet, was reputed to have sighted the *Dutchman*, and it certainly did him no harm for he eventually ascended the throne as King George V.) St. Elmo's fire, a brush discharge of electricity often seen at the masts of ships, was considered to be a benevolent warning of storms. If it was seen to play around the person of a man such as the lookout, however, he would probably die within twenty-four hours.

It is unlucky to whistle aboard a ship, for it will bring a wind, probably blowing foul for the voyage you are on. But if you are becalmed in a sailing vessel, then whistling is useful, and to make sure it blows from the right quarter, stick your jacknife in the mast.

If you encounter a sailor, touch his collar for good luck.

SHRINES AND STATUES

Many religions have established special sites at which the faithful gather to worship, to do reverence to holymen and deities, and to pray for aid or favor.

The church at Broualan, France, was erected in 1483 by a wife whose husband had deserted her. She prayed, and the husband returned. Since then, many abandoned wives have repaired there to pray for the return of their wayward spouses.

A statue of Mateo, the sculptor who designed the portico in the cathedral of Santiago de Compostela, one of the great historic shrines of Christendom, is put to an odd use by Spanish mothers. They bang their children's heads against it, hoping to knock some sense into them.

In Katmandu, Nepal, stands a big red statue to Hanuman, the Monkey God of the epic *Ramayana*, beneath a ceremonial umbrella. Nearby is a stele, centuries old, inscribed in sixteen languages. If you can read them all, superstition says, milk will flow from a tap.

More effective is the statue of Bhairab, God of Fear. Criminals dragged before him to give their testimony believe that, if they lie, they will instantly be struck down. So firm is this belief that many confessions have been exacted there, and some criminals must have lied, for they dropped dead of fright.

But most shrines specialize in cures. A statue in the public fountain at Braga, Portugal, has water flowing from its ears that is believed to improve the hearing of all those drinking it.

At St. Joseph's Oratory in Montreal, many crutches and braces attest to recoveries. This gigantic basilica was erected on its hill in Montreal at the behest of a saintly monk, Brother André, to whose intercession many cures have been attributed. So large is St. Joseph's dome that water condenses on its inner surface and it sometimes "rains" inside.

Asiatics, like Europeans, have many specialized shrines. The tomb of Nasir-ud-Din in Amroha, India, is where you go if you want to recover your ass. (Stray donkeys are supposed to get there eventually.) There are many that offer miraculous cures and spiritual benefits but few that compete with the temple of Arakan, Burma, which guarantees a cure from snakebite if you just touch it. For skin ailments, throw mud at the wall of the temple in Kashgar, Chinese Turkestan.

Perhaps the most famous shrine in the world is that at Lourdes at the foothills of the Pyrenees in southern France. Established in 1858 after a fourteen-year-old peasant girl, Bernadette Soubirous, reported that she had seen the Virgin Mary and been directed to locate a certain spring, the shrine acknowledged fifty "miraculous" cures in its first hundred years. As techniques of diagnosis have become more sophisticated and the authorities more skeptical, the cure rate has slowed down, but now and then a miracle—such as regeneration of dead bone tissue, plainly visible on X rays—is still accepted.

The Roman Catholic Church used to offer indulgences (remission of some punishment for sins that had been confessed and forgiven) for visiting certain shrines. Similarly, in India, anyone who walks around the courtyard of the temple at Tiruvidaimarudur earns merit equal to that of having visited all the other temples of India. Anyone who sees the *chorten* ("shrine") of Tashiding, Sikkim, is immediately cleansed of all sin.

There used to be a gate in Baghdad that the natives believed would give untold wealth to anyone who happened to pass through it at one particular instant in certain twenty-four hour periods. The crowds struggling to take advantage of this opportunity became so unmanageable that the gate had to be bricked up in 1906.

IMAGINARY PLACES

In the days before the globe was as thoroughly explored and mapped as it is today, geographers believed in many dim and distant regions at the rim of Creation. They gave these lands names and locations, and here are some of them.

Atlantis. In two Dialogues, *Timaeus* and *Critias*, Plato mentioned a continent larger than Asia Minor and the known parts of Africa (which would make it about the size of modern Europe). It was reported to lay in the Atlantic Ocean. An idyllic place, perfectly governed, wealthy and peaceful, the island-continent was overwhelmed by jealous aliens and destroyed by earthquakes, but is supposed to lie today somewhere under the sea. Scientists think Plato and his contemporaries may be misremembering the location of an actual island (Mediterranean Thera) that was destroyed by violent volcanic eruptions in 1450 B.C., but other people believe in the literal truth of the story. Some even think the place continues to survive under the sea.

The land of Prester John. Prester (a corruption of the Greek word *presbyter,* "elder") was supposedly a priest-ruler of a mighty Christian empire somewhere in the far reaches of Asia or Africa. There *were* isolated Christian communities in these regions—in Abyssinia (cut off from Christian Europe by the Islamic lands to the north and east), in India (where Christianity was supposedly planted by Saint Thomas the Apostle), and in an area below the Gobi Desert. One of the motivations for early voyages of exploration—motivations at least for the pious monarchs financing them—was to locate the fabled kingdom of Prester John. Long after seamen had brought back facts concerning the Far East and the East Coast of Africa, learned men continued to believe that the land of Prester John lay somewhere out there.

El Dorado. This name actually means "the Gilded Man" and originally referred to a native king of some remote Indian nation who was said to appear on ceremonial occasions with his body covered with gold dust. There actually was a village, located in what is now Colombia, where the chieftain was so decorated at times, but in Indian tales (as they reached Spanish ears) this practice became magnified and rumor persisted of a land so fabuously rich that gold dust was a kind of face powder. For nearly a century this tale lured *conquistadores* high into mountains, deep into jungles, farther and farther from home in search of fabulous wealth. In time "El Dorado" came to mean some mystic land of riches or dreams in quest of which men spent their lives. Even in modern times expeditions have vanished in Latin American jungles, hunting for the Gilded Man and his gold-rich people.

The Northwest Passage. Explorers of the sixteenth and early seventeenth centuries could not bring themselves to believe that what Columbus and his successors had stumbled across was a string of new continents. Rather, South, Central, and North America must be (they thought) a string of islands, like those in the Caribbean. They were convinced in particular that, to the north, there lay a strait—similar to the Strait of Magellan only not situated so far from the temperate climate—that would grant them quick and easy passage to China. The Hudson, the Delaware, and Chesapeake Bay were each in turn thought to be the fabled strait. The French were once convinced that the St. Lawrence would ultimately lead them to the Orient.

Unknown South Land. *Terra Australis Ignota* appeared on many early maps because cartographers felt it *ought* to be there. Surely there had to be something south and west of South America to balance the land masses of the north. Once Australia was discovered, it was named for this supposed land mass, but learned men refused to accept it as a substitute, and *Terra Australis* continued to appear on maps well into the nineteenth century.

5

Events

NEW YEAR'S DAY

Whatever day is celebrated as the first of a new year people regard as a day of fresh beginnings, of expelling old sins and old evils and starting afresh.

In parts of Scotland, it was the custom to usher a dog to the door, give him a piece of bread, and then drive him away, "Get away, you dog!" All the ills that were destined for the following year were supposed to have been laid on the animal's head and thus cast out of the community.

In the Western Himalayas, the Bhotiya people still carry out a similar ceremony. They first feed the dog spirits, bhang (marijuana), and sweets, then lead it around the village, turn it loose, and chase it. When the poor animal is caught and beaten or stoned to death, it is thought that no disease or misfortune will visit the community during the forthcoming year.

Other superstitions in regard to New Year's Day concerned the importance of keeping the fire going. If that was allowed to go out, that was bad luck for the whole year. No neighbor would contribute a coal to start a new one, for that would be giving away her own luck, and to steal fire from someone else was to call even worse luck down on one's head.

Fire was not the only thing that was not to be taken out of the house on New Year's Day. Nothing was to leave—not even refuse.

Another New Year's superstition concerned the British custom of first footing—that is, being the first person to enter the house as the new year dawns. In many parts of Britain it was the custom, as soon as midnight had struck, to make calls on neighbors. If the first footer was a woman, that was bad luck. A fair-haired man was not very popular either, and in parts of the

61

country married men were considered less desirable first footers than bachelors. Ideally, the first footer should be a dark-haired bachelor, and in some communities these lucky individuals made the rounds of all the houses, being warmly welcomed in each. In some regions the first footer was also expected to bring coals, a contribution to keeping the fire going.

In addition it is believed that if your cupboards are bare on New Year's Day, you will have an impoverished year. The same thing holds for being out of money—expect to be broke all year. However, the last drink out of the bottle on New Year's Eve brings good luck to the one who consumes it.

CANDLEMAS, FEBRUARY 2

An ancient Druidic festival was taken over by the Christian Church as the feast of the Purification of the Virgin. It was also the day on which the Church blessed the candles to be used in services throughout the coming year, hence the name "Candlemas." Nevertheless, it—along with its eve, the feast of Saint Brigid—retained many of its old superstitions.

In Scotland, on February 1, women used to dress up a sheaf of oats in women's clothes, lay it in a basket, and say, "Brigid, Brigid, come in—your bed is ready." This Christian saint is thus made to represent the pagan bride of spring, wedded to the soil.

Before Candlemas proper, all Christmas decorations must be removed from the local church. If so much as a leaf or berry is left, the family that occupies the pew where it remains will suffer a death during the next year.

Candlemas was also an important weathercock day. If the sun shone on February 2, it meant a long winter and bad luck. This too:

When the wind's in the east on Candlemas Day,
There it will stick till the second of May.

GOOD FRIDAY

Good Friday beliefs seem to be about equally divided between good luck and bad.

To obtain good luck: Make hot-cross buns; eat some and preserve the rest to prevent whooping cough. (If your husband is a fishermen, have him carry one with him as a safeguard.) Bake bread and save some of it to cure other illnesses; bakings of Good Friday will never go moldy. Have a ring blessed and wear it to prevent illness. Sow parsley, and it will come up double. Move bees only on this day.

To avoid bad luck: Do not hammer iron (it recalls the Crucifixion). Do not put iron into the ground (do not plow or spade up the earth) or nothing will grow in that field that year. Do not hang out clothes, or you will find them spotted with blood.

EASTER

The greatest religious festival of the Christian year, celebrating the Resurrection of Christ, is Easter. But because it comes in the spring, many pre-Christian customs—concerned chiefly with fertility and the renewal of life—have become clustered around it. Hence the many folk beliefs concerning Easter.

Wearing new clothes on Easter will insure good luck for the year. It's not only the rich who follow this tradition and show off their finery in Fifth Avenue's Easter Parade. Sociologists report that, among the very poor, the struggle to obtain new Easter garments for every member of the family often borders on the desperate.

The sun is important in Easter beliefs. At dawn on Easter, many people claim, the sun dances. Others say that at sunrise one can see the Agnus Dei (Lamb of God, a lamb holding a cross or a banner) in the center of the sun. (But don't try looking for it except through smoked glass—gazing directly into the sun can do severe damage to the eyes.) If the sun shines on Easter, it will also shine on Whitsun (Pentecost); if it rains on Easter, it will rain the next seven Sundays, and produce little good hay.

The egg, symbol of new life, is still synonymous with Easter. Decorating Easter eggs is considered a fine art in many parts of Europe, particularly in the Ukraine and Hungary and other parts of Eastern Europe. And in the days of Carl Fabergé (1846–1920), jeweler to Czar Nicholas II, it *was* a fine art, for this gifted goldsmith created enameled and jewel-encrusted Easter eggs that were marvels of beauty and ingenuity.

The ancient Teutons believed that, at Easter, rabbits laid eggs. That's the origin of our Easter bunny. To refuse a gift of an Easter egg was to refuse the friendship of the person offering it. An Easter egg with two yolks meant great prosperity for the fortunate recipient. Eggs blessed at Easter warded off illness. Rolling Easter eggs downhill was a favorite Easter game, the idea being to cross the finish line first with an unbroken shell; if all the eggs were broken, then the winner—who would be rewarded with a year of good luck—was the one whose shell held out longest. The most famous egg rolling today is probably that held on the White House lawn. Few of those who participate, it can be assumed, have any knowledge of the pagan customs dimly recalled in this pleasant occupation.

MAYDAY OR BELTANE

The ancient Druids, or priests of the Celtic peoples of Britain, celebrated four great fire festivals every year equivalent to our Candlemas (February 2), Beltane (May 1), Midsummer (June 23–24), and All Hallows Eve (October 31). Beltane and All Hallows were the big days; then fertility rites were carried out. Giant frameworks of willow were built in the shape of a man, sacrifices of animals and sometimes even human beings were penned up inside them, and they were set afire. Later, in parts of Europe, the wicker effigy was carried in procession as a figure of fun or replaced by young boys dressed in summer greenery who went from house to house collecting fuel for a bonfire. It was called the Beltane fire.

These holidays were often the occasion of much rural mumming and cavorting, people dressing up in masks and costumes and parading about the village. A favorite "character" of such celebrations was the hobby-horse—a crude boat-shaped body of canvas and lath, painted, decorated with ribbons, and topped with a horse's head, which became a central figure in much of the romping. From such antics we derive our term "horseplay."

Mayday superstitions seem to be further survivors of ancient Beltane rites. Washing your face in dew gathered at daybreak on that morning was thought to preserve a woman's complexion. Slavic peasants gathered dew to wash their cows as a preventive against witchcraft. In Spain and France, people rolled naked in dewy grass to protect themselves from skin diseases. Others sniffed it as a cure for vertigo.

If your head is rained on, come May 1, you will have no headaches throughout the year. If you eat sage on Mayday, you will live forever. If you wear a garland, you will find love during the coming year.

On the other hand, cattle were in danger unless you took certain precautions on the first of May. You had to place a green branch against the side of the house or set up a maypole near the cowbarn to ensure plenty of milk. You were well advised to singe cattle with lighted straw on Mayday eve, and bleed them on Mayday itself, the blood then to be burned. You decorated the barn with pieces of rowan. You killed all hares found near the cows, because they were thought to be witches intent on harming the beasts.

In many parts of the world, Beltane fires are still lighted, danced around, and jumped over. In England the celebrations more often feature the maypole, although the dancing nowadays is usually by members of folklore societies, not the simple peasants of former years. The last maypole to be formally erected in London was 130 feet high and took more than four hours to raise with block and tackle. It stood in the Strand for more than half a century, then was taken down in 1717 and sold; Sir Isaac Newton bought it as a support for his new telescope.

WEDDINGS

As one might expect, wedding traditions abound in superstitions, most of them conscientiously followed even by people who would laugh at the notion that they really believe in such things. It would hardly be a proper wedding, they feel, if the bride did not wear "Something old, Something new, Something borrowed, Something blue, With a six pence In her shoe."

Don't get married on February 11, any day in May (it brings poverty), any day in Lent, June 2, November 2 (All Souls' Day), December 1, or December 28 (Holy Innocents' Day). Whatever date you settle on, stick to it. Postponement brings bad luck. "Happy is the bride that the sun shines on," but if it rains go through with the ceremony anyway.

The marriage will be ill-fated . . . if the groom sees the bride on the wedding day, before they meet at church . . . if the bride sees herself in the mirror after she is dressed and before the ceremony . . . if a dog passes between the couple on their wedding day . . . if the wedding party meets a funeral cortege en route to the church . . . if the bride tears her gown or bursts a seam (she will be mistreated by her husband) . . . if it rains . . . if a stone rolls across the path of the newly married pair . . . if the bride stumbles on the threshold of her new home (hence the groom carrying her inside). . . .

The marriage will be happy and blessed . . . if a cat sneezes in the bride's home on the wedding eve . . . if the wedding takes place at the time of the new moon . . . if a hen cackles in the couple's new home . . . if the bride weeps bitterly on her wedding day . . . if the bride wears old shoes . . . if the bridesmaids lay out the bride's stockings (on the wedding night) in the shape of a cross. . . .

It is considered a bad omen if there is an open grave in the churchyard during the wedding ceremony. However, in 1826 in Salisbury, Vermont, when Elizabeth Kelsey married Jonathan Titus, not only was there an open grave but the wedding took place right beside it. The brother of the bride had wanted to attend the nuptials but had died the previous night.

Wedding rings are popular objects of superstition. To cure a stye, rub the ailing eye with a wedding ring. To cure warts, prick them with a gooseberry thorn, thrust through the ring. Turn the ring around three times, and your wish will come true. Never remove the ring except for emergencies. If a wife loses her ring, she will lose her husband; if it breaks, she and her husband will die. A borrowed wedding ring enables an unmarried woman to determine if she will ever marry; suspended over a glass of water from a south-running stream by a hair from her own head, it predicts spinsterhood if it hits the rim of the glass, marriage if it turns quickly around, and two marriages if it revolves slowly.

By the way, it is a popular belief that the ring is worn on the third finger because a vein or a nerve runs from there to the heart. Not so, say Mona and Edmund Radford in their *Encyclopedia of Superstitions*. The third finger is a practical choice, because it is difficult to straighten out unless other fingers are also straightened; thus, since it cannot be extended independently (as all other fingers can, even the pinky) it is the safest finger on which to wear a valuable item of jewelry.

At Jewish weddings, the couple stand under a *huppah*, or wedding canopy, which symbolizes the wedding tent of ancient times. After the bride and groom have both drunk from a wedding glass, it is dropped, and the groom treads on and smashes it, a ceremony that dates back to the fifth century A.D. There are various interpretations of what this symbolizes, perhaps the destruction of the Temple, perhaps simply a reminder that life is fragile. Or perhaps it is to prevent any less happy persons from drinking out of the same fortunate vessel. It has been jokingly suggested that this is included in the wedding ceremony in order to give the husband his last chance to put his foot down. After the glass is broken, the guests cry, "*Mazel*

Tov!" ("Good luck!"), after which the bride, her parents, and her sponsors circle the groom seven times, carrying lighted candles, perhaps marking a mystic, cabalistic circle.

In the Greek Orthodox Church, jeweled crowns are held over the heads of the bride and groom, signifying that the couple are the lord and lady of procreation. They may exchange rings. He receives a gold one; hers is silver.

Many folk beliefs concerning weddings are involved with the struggle to determine which partner will wear the pants in the family. In the Middle Ages, the bridegroom stamped on his new wife's toes. In modern Germany, bride and groom compete to see which one can step on the other's feet, the winner to become dominant. In parts of Britain, the one to retain the mastery will be the one who first steps over the threshold of the church, or the new home.

Wedding cake should be saved by an unmarried young woman and placed under her pillow; she will then dream of her future husband. Whatever she dreams, if dreams come three nights in a row, the third dream will come true.

ASCENSION DAY

This Christian feast, celebrated on a Thursday forty days after Easter, commemorates the ascension of Christ into Heaven.

Rain on Ascension Day portends a poor harvest and sick cattle, but collect the rainwater—it's good for eye troubles. Sunshine, on the other hand, foretells a whole summer of good weather; make a wish as the sun rises. If you do not take a holiday from work on Ascension Thursday, you can expect an accident to occur.

In Saxony peasants used to hold a ceremony called Carrying Out Death. In it a straw effigy (similar to the Scots "Saint Brigid") was dressed in women's clothes, carried through the streets by girls, and then torn apart by boys. In Switzerland, girls climb church towers and ring bells on Ascension Day to ensure a good flax harvest.

BAD DAYS

Numerology, astrology, and almost every other form of superstition believes that people have their good days and their bad days. Arthur

Hopton's *A Concordance of Years*, published in 1612, devotes a whole chapter to "the infortunate and fatall dayes of the years." For instance, in January look out for the first, second, fourth, fifth, tenth, fifteenth, seventeenth, and nineteenth. The *really* "fatall" days are January 3, April 30, July 1, August 1 and 31, and October 7. Hopton says, if you fall ill on one of those days, you will "hardly or never escape."

The following about Evil Days is translated from the Latin of the old Sarum (Salisbury) Missal:

January.	Of this first month, the opening day And seventh like a sword will slay.
February.	The fourth day bringeth down to death; The third will stop a strong man's breath.
March.	The first the greedy glutton slays; The fourth cuts short the drunkard's days.
April.	The tenth, and the eleventh too, Are ready death's fell work to do.
May.	The third to slay poor man hath power; The seventh destroyeth in an hour.
June.	The tenth a pallid visage shows; No faith nor truth the fifteenth knows.
July.	The thirteenth is a fatal day; The tenth alike will mortals slay.
August.	The first kills strong ones at a blow; The second lays a cohort low.
September.	The third day of the month September, And tenth, bring evil to each member.
October.	The third and tenth, with poisoned breath, To man are foes as foul as death.
November.	The fifth bears scorpion-sting of deadly pain; The third is tinctured with destruction's train.
December.	The seventh's a fatal day to human life; The tenth is with a serpent's venom rife.

MIDSUMMER AND MIDSUMMER EVE

The summer solstice usually occurs on June 22 but is celebrated over June 23–24. This recalls the great Druidical festival of Midsummer and is commemorated all across Europe with bonfires and cavortings.

The original intention was to assist the fields to produce a good harvest, and though most such bonfires are considered pure fun today, in some areas they are still lighted so that the smoke blows across the growing crop. In parts of Wales, a cartwheel is wrapped with straw, the straw set afire, and the wheel sent rolling downhill; if it reaches the bottom before the fire goes out, that means the harvest will be a bountiful one.

In some areas, lighted brands were carried through the pastures or the cattle were driven through the smoke. Ashes were later scattered on the crop.

Midsummer Eve is the day on which a girl may meet the man she will later marry. She must fast all day, then at midnight set the table with a clean cloth, bread, cheese, and ale, and sit down as though to eat. Her future husband will then enter and bow to her. Or she must pluck a rose and put it away; if it is still fresh on Christmas Day, she must wear it to church, and her future husband will appear and take it from her.

CORONATIONS

The crowning and annointing of a king has, from ancient times, been a sort of magical ceremony in which the political is united with the sacred and a priest-king is elevated and consecrated. Virtually the sole survivor of this once universal rite is the coronation of British monarchs, a ceremony still retaining much of its ancient beauty and ritual. Naturally many superstitious beliefs have become attached to it.

At his coronation in 1199, King John, an irreverent man, contemptuously threw aside the white spear that symbolized sovereignty over the duchy of Normandy and jeered as they placed the crown of England on his head. A few years later, he lost the duchy in a war with the French king, and eventually, crossing that inlet of the North Sea called The Wash, he was overwhelmed by high tides and lost all his baggage, including the crown.

After his death, he was turned out of his grave by superstitious people, who thought he was a werewolf. *John* is a very common English name, but it is unlikely it will ever be born by another British sovereign. Too unlucky.

James II was crowned on April 23, the feast of Saint George, patron of England. That day in 1685 ought to have been lucky for the new monarch, but the crown, too large, slipped down over James's head, and witnesses interpreted that as a sinister omen. Sure enough, within three years, James was forced to flee his kingdom, to be replaced by his Dutch son-in-law, William III, and his daughter Mary. James's son, called James III by devoted followers and the Old Pretender by his enemies, attempted to regain the throne in 1715 but failed miserably. So did the rebellion in 1745 of the Young Pretender, James II's grandson, affectionately called Bonnie Prince Charlie by the Scots. Thereafter, the Stuart line died out in exile.

And now, of course, Saint George himself has been repudiated by the Roman Catholic Church, one of those early saints whose existence (like that of Nicholas and Christopher) is in doubt.

Against all advice, Charles I wore white, England's unlucky color, at his coronation in 1625. Twenty-four years later, he wound up in another white garment (actually two white shirts, for he was afraid he would be cold and his shivering might be misconstrued as fear) on the scaffold. He was the only British monarch to have his head chopped off—and the most mourned. White used to be the mourning color. Black came later.

At Queen Victoria's coronation in 1838, elaborate preparations were made to assure that all would pass off smoothly. The prime minister had even hidden sandwiches and drinks behind the high altar for his refreshment during the ceremony. But the ring with which the young queen was to wed the nation was too small for the correct finger. Believing that to put it on any but the traditional finger would be unfortunate, the archbishop forced it on her ring finger anyway, and for hours after the ceremony, while others celebrated, she had to sit with her hand in ice water. All the other omens were excellent, however, and her reign was the longest in British history.

After the monarch has been anointed with oil, while the choir sings the Handel anthem "Zadok the Priest," he (or she) is presented to the peers. (In olden days, a king was lifted on a shield and carried aloft.) The peers are asked if they will accept "your undoubted lord," and the traditional response is "God Save the King!" (At the coronation of Edward VII, many peers, so accustomed to Victoria, forgot themselves and shouted, "God Save the Queen!")

At the coronation of one of the Hanoverians, the question was not asked loudly enough, and instead of acclaiming George the king, the crowd of peers was silent. The new monarch looked alarmed, whereat a dowager peeress nearby is said to have electrified Westminister Abbey with the loudest whisper on record: "Does the old fool think with so many drawn swords that anyone will say nay?" This was regarded as an inauspicious beginning for the reign.

MICHAELMAS, SEPTEMBER 29

This feast of Saint Michael the Archangel is associated in Britain with the eating of goose for dinner. As an explanation for this, it is said that Queen Elizabeth I was eating goose on this day when news was brought her of the defeat of the Spanish Armada in 1588, but that can hardly be true, since the Armada had been done away with by the end of July. Whatever the reason, if you eat goose on Michaelmas you will never lack money for the next year.

Michaelmas is also associated with blackberries. In Ireland people claim that on this date the Devil puts his foot on the blackberry, so many people will not pick these berries on the archangel's day.

There is also a folk belief that on Michaelmas Eve at midnight the bracken produces a small blue flower. Actually bracken, a variety of fern, does not flower at all.

The age of the moon—that is, the number of days from the appearance of the new moon—governs the number of days of flood that will follow Michaelmas.

HALLOWEEN OR ALL HALLOWS EVE

The name "All Hallows Eve," which has become worn down to our modern "Halloween," means that it is the eve of All Saints' Day (November 1), when the Church venerates the entire host of those she has canonized as holy. But it coincides in date with the great fall festival of the Druids, in the middle ages was considered one of the great witches' Sabbaths, and today is synonymous with tales of goblins and witches and spooks.

The wind, blowing across corpses, predicts the future on Halloween night. It can be heard sighing against the windows of those who will die within the twelvemonth. If you go to a crossroads and listen to it, you will learn all the things that will happen to you in the coming year. Refine that by sitting at the crossroads on a three-legged stool and wait until the local church clock strikes midnight, and you will hear the names of the parish doomed spoken aloud.

The Irish are particularly strong believers in the evil of Halloween. The dead walk that night, they say; therefore, if you hear footsteps following you, you must not look around for if you meet the glance of the walking dead you will die too. A gambler who wishes to change bad luck to good should hide under a blackberry bush and invoke the aid of the Devil on Halloween; thenceforward he will always win at cards.

In Scotland it's fairies you have to watch out for on Halloween night. Force all your sheep and lambs through a hoop of rowan and make a circuit of the cropland carrying lighted torches.

Much more common, however, are Halloween spells or games to foretell who will be one's mate. A man is advised to crawl under a blackberry bush, and he will see the shadow of his future wife. A girl should wash her chemise and hang it over a chair beside her bed; if she stays awake long enough, the image of her future husband will enter the room and turn the chemise. Or she should take a willow branch in her right hand or a ball of wool yarn, slip out of the house unseen, and run three times around it, saying, "He that is to be my goodman [husband], come and grip." On the third circuit the proper image should appear and take hold of the other end.

Or a girl can stand before a mirror, combing her hair and eating an apple, and her future husband's face will appear in the mirror beside her own. Or she can catch a snail, leave it under a covered dish all night, and next morning see what initial has been traced out by its slimy trail. Or, having peeled an apple, she can throw the peel over her left shoulder; the peel should then form the initial. (It is to be hoped that she has her heart set on someone named Charles or Christopher or whatnot, for apple peels tend to form Cs.)

Apples are important in Halloween lore, particularly in America. A girl can take several apple seeds, give each the name of a potential suitor, place them over or near the fire, and see which is the first to pop; that's the name she wants. Or a group of young people can gather on Halloween night, tie apples to pieces of string, and then whirl them about; the first apple to fall down indicates which person is to be married first. Or each of the group can contribute an apple to a tubful of water and then "bob for apples" (the origin of what is now just a bit of high-spirited horseplay); hands held behind his back, each contestant had to seize an apple in his teeth tightly enough to lift it out (the best way to do this, if one didn't mind ducking, was to pin it against the bottom of the tub), and the person whose apple he managed to catch was his future mate.

HARVEST FESTIVAL

Harvest festivals, in which gratitude is expressed to the life-giving force, whether it is Mother Earth or God the Father, are commonplace throughout the world. Though pagan in origin, they have been taken over by many churches and modern religions. The Jewish feast of Tabernacles, Sukkoth, is still celebrated by many Jews with the setting up of tentlike structures in backyards or in houses or on the balconies of apartment buildings and the setting out of harvest fruits. Every autumn in Britain, parish churches are still decorated with produce of the fields, and a special service is held, at which the congregation sings:

> All good gifts around us
> Are sent from Heaven above,
> So thank the Lord, thank the Lord
> For all His love.

This pagan festival was resurrected in the Church of England in the 1840s by the Reverend R. S. Hawker, who served a remote parish in Cornwall. In their Celtic past, Cornishmen had sacrificed to the Druids' gods of fertility by sprinkling blood in the fields. Mr. Hawker revived this ancient attitude toward the fruits of the earth, giving it the sanction of the Church.

But this does not mean that unabashedly pagan beliefs concerned with the harvest do not still abound. To have a big crop next year, make the last sheaf of harvest a big one. For good luck, make sure one sheaf is bound by a woman. Make a corn baby (a symbolic image out of straw) and set it up in the house.

Many American communities still hold Harvest Home festivals, although this is usually combined with Halloween parties. In the past it was popular to celebrate with a corn-shucking bee. Before the advent of corn hybridization, an occasional red-kerneled ear (nicknamed "Indian corn") would turn up in a crop of normal yellow ears. It was considered highly lucky to find such an ear; it won you a kiss from your sweetheart, and you saved it until the following harvest as a charm. Today people may buy colored ears at the supermarket and affix them to their front doors.

Some people consider the American festival of Thanksgiving as a kind of harvest festival. However, its late date (the original was held in December, 1621, and the modern feast has been established as the fourth Thursday in November) make it unsuitable for a celebration of harvest. Moreover, there seem to be few superstitions in connection with it.

DAYS OF BIRTH

From the days of the ancient cave dwellers to today's earnest followers of astrological horoscopes, the time of a child's birth has been held to be of major importance to its life. Here are some folk beliefs concerning births.

Bad days to be born: March 21, any day between June 23 and July 23, any day in May.

Good days to be born: Sundays, New Year's Day, Christmas Day. The last is particularly desirable, because the child will be psychic. A child born on Sunday cannot be harmed by evil spirits. Many people know this old rhyme:

> Monday's child is fair of face;
> Tuesday's child is full of grace;
> Wednesday's child is full of woe;
> Thursday's child has far to go;
> Friday's child is loving and giving;
> Saturday's child works hard for a living;
> And the child that is born on the Sabbath day
> Is blithe and bonny, good and gay.

Natural phenomena control the good/bad luck of birth. People who live by the seaside believe that a child is not likely to be born until the tide is in (just as old people are not likely to die until the tide is out), and if it is born during the ebb, it will not live long. It is better to be born at night than during the day, especially if the moon if full (if you are born in the dark of the moon, you will not live past puberty). In Sicily it is believed that girls are born under a waning moon and boys under a waxing one. A child born at midnight will be able to see the spirits of the departed. Sunrise is a lucky time to be born, for the child will have a long life; a sunset birth means the child will be lazy.

CHRISTMAS EVE

Christmas is so popular a holiday that whole books have been written about the customs, beliefs, and superstitions connected with it.

Things to do for good luck: Tie wet straw around the fruit trees, so that they will yield well the following year. Bring holly into the house (bad luck if you bring it before this). Hang up mistletoe for a good-luck kiss and after New Year's Day give it to the first cow that calves. (Warning: mistletoe must be burned before Twelfth Night, January 6, or all the couples who kissed under it will be enemies before the end of the year.) At midnight, open the doors and windows to let out evil spirits and welcome in the good.

Things to avoid to escape bad luck: Cutting the Christmas cake before Christmas Eve. Allowing fire or a light to leave the house.

Advice to unmarried girls: Walk backward to the nearest pear tree, walk around it nine times, and see an image of your husband-to-be. Go to the henhouse and tap sharply; if a cock crows first, you will be wed within the year, and if a hen cackles, you won't. Go into the garden at midnight, pick twelve sage leaves, and glimpse the shadowy form of your future husband. Silently make a dough cake, prick your initials in it, and place it on the hearth; at midnight, a vision of your husband-to-be will enter and prick his initials beside yours. Get engaged—very good luck will follow.

Special sights at midnight: All cattle kneeling and lowing. Bees humming the Hundredth Psalm. The rosemary bursting into flower. Familiar faces appearing in the flames of the Yule log. (But if those flames cast headless shadows, beware. The persons whose shadows those are will die before the year is out.)

By the way, never mind what Dickens says in *A Christmas Carol*— ghosts absolutely never appear on Christmas Eve.

CHRISTMAS DAY

Don't go out of the house until a dark man has come to visit (a form of first footing). If a woman appears first, that's very bad luck. Don't turn the mattress. When it's time to go out, wassail the apple trees with cider.

Christmas predictions: A child born on Christmas will never be hanged. If the sun shines through an apple tree on Christmas Day, it will be heavy with fruit next year. Light Christmas, light wheatsheaves; dark Christmas, heavy wheatsheaves (if Christmas is an overcast day, there will be an abundant harvest).

Our symbols of Christmas have come to us from many lands. Mistletoe was venerated by the Druids, especially as it grew on the oak, which was sacred to them. Druids distributed sprigs of mistletoe to people, who hung up these evergreen branches in hope that the nature deities would restore greenery in the spring. A similar reason governed the use of holly and ivy, considered to represent male and female respectively. A fifteenth-century carol depicts a debate between the two over which one held the mastery; it concludes with Holly yielding gracefully.

> Then spake Holly and set him down on his knee,
> "I pray thee, gentle Ivy, say me no villainy,
> In Landes where we goe."

The Yule log comes from Scandinavia, where it was burned as a kind of winter-solstice purification rite. Origin of the word *Yule* is in dispute, but one theory claims that it meant an ancient Teutonic winter season, roughly mid-November to mid-January. Christians took over the practice and made great merriment over dragging it into the hall with singing and dancing. Robert Herrick tells us that for good luck the Yule log had to be lighted from a brand of the previous year's log:

> Kindle the Christmas brand, and then
> Till sunset let it burn,
> Which quenched, then lay it up again,
> Till Christmas next return.

The Yule log crossed the Atlantic and became part of American Christmas traditions, especially in the South. Slaves were allowed to keep holiday as long as the log burned, so it was always thoroughly soaked before being lighted and carefully tended to keep it smoldering for days.

The wassail bowl is an ancient Anglo-Saxon tradition. Carolers carried cups with them, and wherever they stopped to serenade neighbors they held out the cups and cried, "Wassail! Wassail!" At that the family being serenaded was expected to fill the cups with "lambswool," a hot spiced ale with roasted apples floating in it. "You may have it of the costliest wine, or the humblest malt liquor," wrote Leigh Hunt. "But in no case must the roasted apples be forgotten."

And last, but far from least, is the Christmas tree, a relatively recent import from Germany. It did not arrive in Great Britain until Queen Victoria married Prince Albert of Saxe-Coburg (Germany), but it reached American shores a good 150 years earlier than that with the first German settlers. Lighted by small candles (modern Germans still prefer them to electric tree lights), decorated with trinkets and little figures, surrounded by presents, surmounted by a star or an angel figure, it is still the heart of the family's celebration of this most beloved of holidays.

OTHER SPECIAL OCCASIONS

Epiphany or Three Kings' Day, January 6. Take down the Christmas tree. Make a cake containing a ring and a button; whoever gets the ring will marry during the year, and whoever gets the button will not.

Valentine's Day, February 14. Write the names of your boyfriends on bits of paper, stick each one into a ball of clay and drop them into water; the one that rises first will contain your true love's name.

Mardi Gras or Shrove Tuesday (the last day before the start of Lent). Make pancakes for the family and throw one to a rooster. If he eats it all, expect bad luck. If the hens get most of it, good luck will be yours.

Ash Wednesday (first day of Lent). Eat pea soup. Do not sell any cattle.

Lent (forty days of fasting and repentance that precede Easter). "Marry in Lent, live to repent." Until very recently, many Christian churches forbade couples to marry during Lent and Advent.

St. Swithin's Day (July 15). If it rains today, it will rain for the forty days that follow. Swithin was bishop of Winchester, and before he died (in 862) he requested that he be buried outdoors under "the sweet rain of heaven." This request was carried out, but later (when he was canonized) the monks of the nearby abbey tried to move him indoors to a grander tomb (this was on July 15), but it started to rain and did not stop for forty days, so they took that as a sign of the saint's displeasure and returned him to his original grave.

All Souls' Day (November 2). As the previous day commemorated All Saints, so this day commemorated the rest of the dead, and it was believed that all souls still suffering in Purgatory were released for twenty-four hours. If at midnight two people walk around a room in total darkness, in opposite directions, they will never meet and one will be spirited away.

PART TWO

The Future

"The Only Way to Predict the Future Is to Have the Power to Shape the Future"

THE black magician, turning to necromancy, attempts to raise evil spirits in order to learn their deepest secrets, including the nature of the future. With terrifying ceremony, he sacrifices a stolen baby and prays:

> Astoreth, Asmodeus, principles of friendship and love, I invoke you to accept as sacrifice this newborn child that I offer you for the things I ask; and that you will deny me nothing in return for this offering, whether for myself, my relatives, or any of my household.

Other men cast horoscopes in hopes of uncovering the great truths of nature and seeing into the future. They read tea leaves, dice, or cards; feel bumps on heads and pore over lines in palms; explore omens and auguries, the Tarot or the *I Ching*. They interpret dreams. They study the peculiarities of chance. They strive to peer beyond the veil of Death itself.

Astrology, the "science" that is studied by more Americans today than any that operate on heavy government funding, goes back to the stargazers of ancient Chaldea. It supplied a good part of early science and the occult lore of masonry, theosophy, and other movements. We may have gone beyond it but we are peculiarly reluctant to leave it behind.

Our traditions of fortune-telling are likewise long-lived, coming to us along with the rest of our culture essentially from our pagan past. Romans, hard-headed though they were in other ways, believed implicitly in fortune-telling and kept state augurs to examine the entrails of animals and the flight of birds and thus predict what was good for the state and what wasn't.

Luck, on the other hand, though believed in almost universally from the beginning of time, has only recently begun to be studied by mathematicians, sociologists, and others interested in the vagaries of chance. Nonetheless, the thing itself has been wooed and fretted over since man lived in caves and learned how to make fire.

Like fortune-telling, interpretation of dreams goes far back into the misty past, inspiring many writers of classical times and earlier to expatiate on what dreams mean. In the Bible, Joseph interprets Pharaoh's dream about cattle. In *The City of God*, Saint Augustine explains the meaning of sexual nightmares.

As for death, when has man not speculated on the meaning of it and what will become of him when his earthly body decays?

In this section, we explore those forms of occult thought that have occupied wonderers from the beginning of time.

6

Predictions and Prophecies

LOOK, WE'VE COME THROUGH!

In just the last few decades, the end of the world has been fairly often predicted. In mid-January 1976, a man named John Nash caused quite a stir in Adelaide, Australia, by predicting that the city, perhaps the world, would soon be destroyed by a giant tidal wave.

Some Aussies fled to the hills, but the prime minister and a host of other optimists gathered on the beach to celebrate what turned out to be the Big Non-Event. Adelaide is still there. So is California, despite dire predictions ("Buy some beach property now in Nevada"), and so is the great Globe itself, despite the men with the signs saying, "The End Is Nigh." We can, in fact, expect many more dire warnings of the Holocaust and Armageddon and nuclear disintegration and so on.

By rights, one of these many predictions of disaster, just by the law of averages, actually ought to coincide with a real event. It is really remarkable that it hasn't. After all, in Tacoma, Washington, a vast bridge was blown down, in Wales a pile of mine dumpings collapsed and smothered a village school, balconies plunged to the lobby of a modern hotel in Kansas City, there have been many calamitous oil spills, and numerous other manmade catastrophes have occurred—not to mention such Acts of God as volcanic eruptions, earthquakes, tidal waves, floods, hurricanes, tornadoes, and the rest. And yet no one warned the public that these specific cataclysms were on the way.

The next Big One to watch out for is the end of the world in the year 2000. Scientists say the world will last to the year 10,000,000,000; the superstitious say no.

81

A USEFUL VISION

Sometimes clairvoyant episodes stem from the close personal relationships between two persons. *Phantasms of the Living*, a famed collection of such incidents, tells, for example, about a child of ten who, while away from home, had a sudden vision of her mother lying on the floor. The child fetched the doctor, and they ran to the house, where they found the mother exactly as she had been "seen." Their promptness saved her life. "The account does not add," comments novelist Colin Wilson, "that there was a strong bond between mother and daughter, but there undoubtedly was."

A THEORY OF THE SUPERNATURAL

One of the most convincing theories about what makes parapsychological episodes possible occurs not in a learned tome but in a short story—"The Bus Conductor" by E. F. Benson, a literate student of the occult and son of an archbishop of Canterbury.

Imagine then that you and I and everybody in the world are like those people whose eye is directly opposite a little tiny hole in a sheet of cardboard which is continually shifting and revolving and moving about. Back to back with that sheet of cardboard is another, which also, by laws of its own, is in perpetual but independent motion. In it, too, there is another hole, and when, fortuitously it would seem, these two holes, the one through which we are always looking, and the other in the spiritual plane, come opposite to one another, we see through, and then only do the sights and sounds of the spiritual world become visible and audible to us. With most people these holes never come opposite each other during their life. But at the hour of death they do, and then they remain stationary. That, I fancy, is how we "pass over."

If Benson's theory has some validity, could it be that some people are able to get these "holes" to coincide frequently? If so, it would explain that mysterious power of "second sight" that other people can hardly credit.

MUZA'S FATE

Mlle. Irene Muza of the Comédie Française predicted her own death. And she never knew she had done so.

"My career will be short," she wrote in a trance; no unusual life for an actress, it must be admitted, but she added: "I dare not say what my end will be. It will be terrible."

It was. A few months later Mlle. Muza was accidentally set on fire by her hairdresser; she perished in the flames.

The trance-state prediction had been kept from her by kind friends. But it came true, nevertheless.

FATAL ACCURACY

The German astronomer and astrologer David Fabricius (1546–1617) predicted in 1607 that he would die ten years later; the date he "saw" was May 7, 1617. On that day in 1617 he stayed home with his doors and windows locked, but at midnight he thought he was safe and ventured a walk in his garden. He was set upon by a maniac he had never seen before, who split his skull open with a pitchfork.

PORTENTS

Shakespeare often mentions portents: a lion in the street the night before the death of Julius Caesar, the strange goings-on indicative of the reversal of order presaging the death of King Duncan in *Macbeth*, and so on. Here is a real case, as reported by John Aubrey in his *Miscellanies*:

When King James II first entered Dublin after his arrival from France in 1689, one of the Gentlemen that bore the Mace before him, stumbled without any rub [obstacle apparent] in his way, or other visible occasion. The Mace fell out of his hands, and the little Cross upon the Crown thereof stuck fast between the [cobble] stones in the Street. This is well known all over Ireland, and did much trouble King James himself with many of his chief Attendants.

That the son of James I (who staunchly defended the existence of witchcraft against Reginald Scot's *Discouerie of Witchcraft*, which declared it a delusion) believed in this is perhaps not remarkable. What is notable is that so many other people would take this accident as a portent foretelling the fall of the king. Superstition was rampant among the Jacobites and the Anti-Jacobites alike, so that a thing like that could be bad propaganda indeed.

NIXON AND DIXON

Prognosticator Jean Dixon said in *Parade* on May 13, 1956, that "a blue-eyed Democratic President elected in 1960 will be assassinated." There are many evidences that President Kennedy was told not to drive through Dallas that fateful day, too. But Miss Dixon in 1960 also predicted that Richard Nixon would beat John Kennedy in the election. Neither that nor her prediction of World War III (slated for 1958) came true. The assassination did.

My favorite prediction is the one (not by Miss Dixon) that President Nixon would come to grief over "a piece of tape." Some friends and myself got this one with a Ouija board two years before Watergate (and were wrong by a whole year about the date). When the news of Watergate broke, I thought the White House recorded tapes made the prediction look very important. Later I realized that the "piece of tape" that really brought the President down was the little piece that the Watergate plumbers put over a lock in the offices of the Democrats they were burgling. If *that* had not been noticed by a nightwatchman . . .

SMALL CHANGE

The Maoris still believe that in reciting a spell one little slip of the tongue can be fatal. In Europe it was often said that the smallest error in a spell or magical ceremony would invalidate the whole thing. I have been told by several ritual magicians that the reason certain ceremonies did not work for me was that I sang the magical words to the wrong notes. Had I been better able to carry a tune, I might now be both rich and invisible.

WHAT DO YOU HEAR?

Here's a method for getting news of the future (or the answer to any pressing question). According to Greek geographer Pausanias, it was used at a shrine of Hermes, that of Apollo at Thebes, and that of Zeus at Olympia. The Greeks swore by it.

You went up to the statue of Hermes, lighted the bronze lamps on the hearth-altar (rather like burning a candle in church), put a coin on the altar, and whispered your question into the statue's ear. Then you clapped your hands over your own ears and walked away. The first speech you heard on taking your hands away from your ears was your clue to the answer.

Maybe you'd like to forecast the financial market by using the statue of George Washington on the steps of the U.S. Sub-Treasury building in New York. Run straight over to the Stock Exchange to unblock your ears. This system may work as well as any on Wall Street.

JEWISH DIVINATION

In Biblical times, the Jews believed in official divination to determine the future and the will of God. When officiating at sacred functions, the High Priest wore the ephod, an apronlike vestment, and over it the breastplate of righteousness, or *hoshen*. This breastplate displayed four rows of three stones each, representing and inscribed with the names of the Twelve Tribes of Israel: sardius for Reuben, topaz for Simeon, carbuncle for Judah, emerald for Dan, sapphire or lapis lazuli for Naphtali, diamond or crystal for Gad, jacinth (an orangish stone) for Asher, agate for Issachar, amethyst for Zebulun, beryl for Benjamin, onyx for Manasseh, and jasper for Ephraim. Underneath the *hoshen*, over the priest's heart, was a pouch, sometimes called the pocket of decision, which contained the mysterious Urim and Thummim, sacred lots used for divination or reading the oracles. It is uncertain today exactly what they were or how they worked.

It was when Saul could obtain no information from Urim and Thummim—or from dreams or prophets—that he turned to the witch of Endor to learn why he was out of favor with the Lord (I Samuel 28: 6–19). Magicians who use "the powers" of precious and semiprecious stones today will tell you the ancient Hebrews went about it in the wrong way in arranging these stones; no wonder they didn't work, they say.

YOUR BABY'S FUTURE

Put out a Bible, a silver dollar, and a pack of cards. If the baby touches the Bible, he will be a preacher. If he picks up the silver dollar, he will be a financier. If he touches the pack of cards, he will turn out to be a gambler.

If he picks up all three, perhaps when he grows up he will take a chance on becoming a money-grubbing TV evangelist! Or such is the facetious claim of some people.

OGMA

Ogma was the Celtic god of fertility and healing, of eloquence and prophecy. He is credited with the invention of the Ogham alphabet.

POLYNESIAN PROPHECIES

In Polynesia they set up sticks, each one representing a tribesman, and judged thereby which of their warriors would fall in battle. They also spun coconuts to catch thieves.

DIVINING RODS

Divining rods were once used in France to track criminals or heretics, but a law of 1701 forbade their employment and such evidence was thereafter not admitted in court. Today psychics are occasionally used in trying to track down criminals or find lost persons.

THE END OF THE WORLD

Christianity has been plagued by no end of end-of-the-worldists. In the second century, it was Montanism (a sect of extreme asceticism) that claimed, among other things, that the New Jerusalem (the next world) was soon to appear at the sect's headquarters in Phrygia. The world did not end when predicted, of course, but Montanism continued to gather converts. In the third century, it made its only important one, the ecclesiastical writer Tertullian, but later Church Fathers (such as Origen and Clement of Alexandria) were unimpressed, and eventually the Emperor Justinian proscribed the sect. The Montanists thereupon locked themselves in their churches and set fire to them. That really was the end of the world—for them, at least.

The millenarians forecast the end of the world for the year 1000. They were wrong, too. Neo-millenarians look bleakly toward the year 2000.

POLITICAL PROGNOSTICATION

In 1213 Peter the Wise, a Yorkshire hermit, was hanged because he predicted the death of King John. Treason as well as sorcery, they said—not wise of him at all. In 1580 Elizabeth I passed a law against foretelling the death of the monarch. At that time, rumors such as that could be a lot of help to fomenters of rebellion, such as Mary, Queen of Scots. Mary was well aware of the usefulness of prophecy as propaganda, and she herself called it "the very Foundation of all Rebellion."

The connection of sorcery with politics is a book in itself. I predict someone will attempt it soon.

PREMONITIONS

Everyone has many premonitions; most of them never come true. But every time some spectacular event hits the headlines there are people who claim that they saw it coming all along.

Next time you have a strong premonition, why not get it on record *before* the event? Then you'll find researchers in this field far more interested in it as evidence.

In New York, contact the American Society for Psychical Research, Box 482, Times Square Station, New York, New York 10036. In London, you can write or telegraph the Central Premonitions Register (at the *Evening Standard*) or the Society for Psychical Research, Adam and Eve Mews, London W8.

FATALISM

Che sera, sera ("Whatever will be, will be") is one of the world's most widespread beliefs. Before King Abdullah of Jordan was assassinated in Jerusalem in 1951, he used to quote an Arab proverb: "Until my day comes, nothing can hurt me; when my day comes, nothing can save me." He was right.

Magic, of course, attempts to change events, to force Heaven to its own will. Magic is never satisfied with the idea of things just happening; it wants to *make* things happen. It never pauses to consider that what magicians and seers do is also, perhaps, part of the Great Plan—all dictated from on high, all foreseen and ordained.

COMEUPPANCE

In the year 1370, the road to Canterbury was choked with pilgrims on their way to the shrine of Saint Thomas à Becket. The traffic jam inconvenienced the bishop of London, Simon Sudbury, and he cried out to the throng: "Plenary indulgence for your sins by repairing to Canterbury? Better hope might ye have of Salvation had ye stayed at home. . . ."

Thomas of Aldon, a Kentish squire, was outraged that the bishop should insult England's favorite saint. He shouted back: "My lord bishop . . . I will give up my own salvation if you yourself do not die a most shameful death!"

Eleven years later, Sudbury had attained the highest rank in the English Church, archbishop of Canterbury. But that did not save him. In the Wat Tyler commotions of 1380–81, he was attacked by a mob and ignominiously beheaded on Tower Hill.

The Kentishman did not have to give up his own salvation as offered, for his prophecy, or curse, had come true.

PROPHECIES OF DOOM

English history is full of dire warnings. As a boy King Richard III was warned by a soothsayer that he would die "soon after he gazed upon

Rougemont." One day in 1485 he was startled to learn that a castle he had paused to admire was called Rougemont. A few weeks later, he was slain at Bosworth Field. Many lies were told to and about the enigmatic Richard, but this prophecy seems to have been one important truth.

Thomas Cardinal Wolsey (1475–1530), chancellor of capricious Henry VIII, was warned by a fortune-teller that "Kingston" would mark the end of his life. He deliberately avoided that town name from then on, and on one occasion, when under the king's displeasure, he even gave Henry his glorious palace at Hampton Court in an attempt to placate fate. But one day when the cardinal was ill and worried, a constable arrived, sent by Henry. Wolsey is said to have died of shock on learning that the man's name was Kingston.

CASANOVA'S PROPHECY

Giovanni Casanova (1725–98), who is known chiefly for his sexual conquests, also indulged occasionally in prophecy. One instance involved Sir Thomas Hope, a wealthy merchant, whom Casanova convinced of a vision in which he saw a ship of Hope's. It was heavily laden and safe at sea, although others had given it up for lost. The ship did indeed come in, and Casanova was well rewarded.

Of course, had it been lost, Casanova would have had to make still another of his many midnight departures from foreign cities. As it was, he had all Amsterdam talking about his ability to see into the future, a useful talent in marine insurance.

AN IRISH OCCURRENCE

A story is told of an Irishman who lay down in a field to sleep and who, waking, found himself both deaf and dumb. He could signal messages to his friends, however, and he told them many wonderful things he had never known when he was in possession of all his faculties. He could foretell the future and knew instantly of events at great distances.

In time he recovered his ordinary abilities to hear and speak and in that instant he lost all his paranormal powers. He never could explain what had happened to him.

Think about this story in terms of the folk wisdom enshrined in superstitions, the deep truth of primitive legends, the unsophisticated but subtle insights in the short and simple annals of the poor.

ROYAL PROPHECIES

King Philip II of Macedonia, warned by an oracle to "beware of a chariot," thereafter staunchly refused to ride in one. But at his daughter's wedding (336 B.C.) he was slain by an assassin whose dagger hilt was decorated with a carving of a chariot.

When the mosque of the Sultan Hassan in Cairo was under construction in 1329, a soothsayer warned the monarch that completion of a second minaret would cause his death. He ordered the building to proceed. The second minaret stood, and he congratulated himself on his wisdom. In 1361 that minaret crashed down on an adjacent orphanage, killing three hundred children. They say that when the sultan died thirty-three days later, it was of a broken heart.

When Louis XV attended divine service on March 31, 1774, Bishop Jean de Beauvais (1731–1790) took as the text of his sermon Jonah 3:4: "Yet forty days and Nineveh shall be overthrown." Exactly forty days later Louis XV was dead.

Constantine the Great prophesied that the number 13 would bring down Constantinople. It was eleven hundred years later, when Constantine XIII was Byzantine emperor (he was actually only the eleventh of that name, but some early historians called him XIII) that the Turks destroyed the city. That was in 1453. If you add 1, 4, 5, and 3 the total is 13.

BLAKE THE MYSTIC

Some of the very best English mystical poetry is from the pen of William Blake, the early Romantic poet who not only had visions that he built into such works as *The Book of Thel* and *The Four Zoas* but also claimed he chatted with an archangel in his back garden. He had other psychic experiences. In 1771, as a youth of fourteen, he was apprenticed to William Rylands, then England's foremost engraver, to learn the art of etching. The job lasted only one day, because young Blake could not stand the fact that whenever he looked at his master he saw Rylands dangling dead on a gallows.

It was twelve years before this prophetic vision was explained. Rylands was hanged for forgery on August 29, 1783.

NOSTRADAMUS

It was Merlin, magician at the court of the legendary King Arthur, who is supposed to have said that he would "not speak before our people nor at court save in obscure words, nor will they know what I mean until they see it come to pass." One Michel de Nôtre-Dame (1503–1566) was the past master of this particular form of prognostication. You know him better by his Latin name, Nostradamus.

Though he was named for the Blessed Virgin, Nostradamus came from a long line of Jewish physicians. His grandfather was physician to King René of Anjou. The family converted to Christianity and took the Christian surname "Nôtre-Dame." In spite of the anti-Semitism that raged in Europe in the fifteenth century (and led to the expulsion of the Jews from Spain in 1492), Christian communities experienced a heavy influx of Jewish magic and scientific learning.

Science and magic were then mixed, and Nostradamus, who had a degree in medicine from Montpellier, gained himself a reputation (as did the famous Dr. Faustus) fighting an epidemic of the plague. Like many another physician and banker in the period, he traveled far and wide and picked up extra money spying; Nostradamus was a spy for the kingdom of France and for the duchies of Savoy and Lorraine.

Another sideline was astrology and prediction. In 1555 he published *Centuries*, a book of rhymed prophecies, and attracted the patronage of the powerful queen, Catherine de Médicis, herself no mean plotter and dabbler in the occult.

For her he prophesied:

> The young lion shall overcome the old,
> On the field of war, in mortal combat.
> He will pierce his eyes in a cage of gold.
> This is the first of two loppings, then he dies a cruel death.

How's that for obscure? Yet two years later it seemed crystal-clear. In a joust Catherine's husband, Henri II, celebrating the marriage of his daughter, ran against the earl of Montgomery, and the earl's lance pierced the grille of Henri's golden helmet. He died after ten days of excruciating pain caused by a piece of the lance lodged in his eye.

Catherine was interested. She had always wanted to know about the future (and plots, poisons, and other things useful in politics). Anyone who could predict an accident like that could be useful. After forty-five sittings with Nostradamus, Catherine (it is claimed) was visited by an angel who told her everything that would happen to her family, including the fact that the assassination of Henri III would put an end to the dynasty of the Valois—as indeed it did, eventually.

Ordinarily Nostradamus did not produce such extraordinary messen-. gers or such clear-cut messages. He dealt in "obscure words" which were then read, and read into. It was said he predicted World War I, but the prophecy did not seem to mean much until World War I had already begun. In World War II both the British and the Nazis used the ambiguity of Nostradamus's prophecies for propaganda purposes, "reading" them to suit themselves.

If you would like to try interpreting him, there are still many prophecies left dealing with events yet to come, and his 333 quatrains are a lot more readily available today than they ever were in his own time. He is something of a best-selling author in this field.

One quatrain discusses "the Oriental" who is to "pass through the sky" and start what looks like World War III in the very late twentieth century, unless that meant Pearl Harbor in World War II! But if Nostradamus is right, World War III will not be the total annihilation everyone else is talking about, for his prophecies end with A.D. 3797, which means presumably that the world still has some time to run.

THE DEVIL TO PAY

If you want to look into the future, it can be expensive. Remember that Dr. Faustus had to sell his soul to the Devil and then was cheated, too. In the *Rituale Romanum*, liturgical manual for the Roman Catholic Church, the third instruction on exorcism says (in Latin) that a possessing devil reveals himself by the ability of the possessed person to "reveal distant or hidden things." Also, "There are uncountable tricks and frauds that the devil will use to deceive."

Are you sure you wouldn't prefer just to wait and see what happens?

STILL WORKING ON THE CAYCE

To many Americans, Edgar Cayce, the controversial miracle man of Virginia Beach, Virginia, is the prophet par excellence. Nearly forty years after his death (in 1945) the paperback racks of bookstores are crammed with various volumes devoted to his healing arts and prognostications.

The most disturbing prophecy he made concerns the destruction of a great part of the western United States by earthquakes, an event Cayce said would occur in this century and be accompanied by the destruction of much of Europe and Japan.

Undeterred, Americans are flocking west in greater and greater numbers; people from the Frost Belt have been moving to the Sun Belt, the East Coast is losing out to the West Coast. How long this can go on will soon be seen, for Cayce's prophecies speak of the 1990s as the bad times. By the turn of the century New York, too, would be under water, the prophet claimed.

Cayce diagnosed diseases at a distance (over 14,000 cases) merely by going into a trance. Many people credit him with amazing cures. He also undertook to tell people about their "previous lives," for he firmly believed in reincarnation. He gave elaborate, detailed history of the lost city of Atlantis. He predicted that "the temple will rise again" and that "Poseidia will be among the first portions of Atlantis" to be rediscovered. "Expect it in 1968 or 1969," he said (in 1934), and in 1968 ruins that some believed to be the pillars of a massive temple were found off the coast of Bimini in the Caribbean.

ACE OF SPADES

In cartomancy, or fortune-telling by cards, the Ace of Spades relates to love. When it is accompanied by the 10 of Spades, you can expect a lot of trouble. If it appears upside down, the Ace of Spades means pregnancy, and if the Knave of Clubs is also reversed, death. Bad news all around.

PROGNOSTICATION

If you want to find out how the American Federation of Astrologers is going to fare as an organization, you might try making a horoscope for it. Its birth time was May 4, 1938, and the place Washington, D.C.

GROUNDS FOR BELIEF

You have heard of tea-leaf readers. In Macedonia they tell the future from coffee grounds. And in France, using coffee grounds, Mme. Bontemps told the fortunes of Mme. de Pompadour, the duc de Choiseul, and other court figures—with what accuracy I am not sure, but they were satisfied.

THALES

Thales of Miletus, Greek philosopher of the sixth century B.C., requested that at his death he be buried in a certain obscure corner of his native city, for that lonely spot would one day become the forum or center of town. He was, and it did.

HAVE A NICE YEAR

What's going to happen this year, a Chinese astrologer will tell you, has something to do with which of the creatures happens to rule this period. The twelve-animal, twelve-year cycle goes like this:

Rat	Horse
Ox	Goat
Tiger	Monkey
Cat	Rooster
Dragon	Dog
Snake	Pig

1983-5744

The Jewish year beginning in September 1983 is numbered 5744. In traditional Jewish numerology, this spells *DOOM*. "Sheer and utter super-

stitious nonsense," says Dr. Ronald Sobel, rabbi of New York's Temple Emmanuel. If you are Jewish, however, and not Reformed, go worry.

WHAT IS NEEDED

William James, brother of novelist Henry James, was one of the main forces behind the founding in 1885 of the American Society for Psychical Research. As a philosopher, James was interested in new ideas. As a psychologist, he was aware of human gullibility. As a practical scientist, he wanted hard facts. He used to say, "To upset the conclusion that all crows are black, there is no need to seek demonstration that no crow is black; it is sufficient to produce one white crow."

To acknowledge that occult power is at work in some prophets, the world needs at least one list of absolutely specific predictions, all of which come true. That would convince the hardest-nosed statistician and others that the gift for accurate prognostication goes far beyond the so-called laws of probability.

But we are a long way from having it. Every year the *National Enquirer* and other popular papers are chock full of predictions (usually about what entertainment personality is soon to be married or divorced), but the trouble is that most of these prognostications do not come true. When one of them does turn out to be accurate, it is unlikely that anything more than guesswork or chance was behind it.

PRECOGNITION

Can people know things before they happen? Well, everyone has had a hunch from time to time, but some people have experiences of elaborate precognition—rare, hard to explain, and apparently pointless. In 1926 British psychic researcher Dr. S. G. Soal reported just such an incident in *Proceedings of the Society for Psychical Research*. Four years earlier, Dr. Soal was taking part in a séance with the medium Blanche Cooper when he received a "message" purportedly from Gordon Davis, an old school friend of Soal's.

The spirit voice spoke of a row house in "half a street" with *E* somehow important; the house had five or six steps "and a half" leading up to it and a "funny dark tunnel" beside it. Opposite the house was "something" the other houses did not have but "not a veranda."

Inside the house, the voice said, an upstairs room had a very large mirror and pictures of "glorious" mountains and seascapes. Some very large vases and "funny saucers" were mentioned. Downstairs there were "two funny brass candlesticks" and a "black dickie-bird on the piano." A wife and a small son were mentioned.

At the time of the séance, Dr. Soal was under the impression that his old friend Gordon Davis had been killed in action in World War I. So what was this row house? Was it in the next world, or what?

Three years later Dr. Soal discovered that his friend was still in this world—and so was the house. It was located at 54 Eastern Esplanade, Southend-on-Sea, and Gordon Davis was living at that address.

On April 18, 1925, Dr. Soal went to visit his friend in Southend. The house at 54 Eastern Esplanade (the "important" *E*) faced the seafront, with a promenade shelter right across the street (apparently the "something" other houses did not have) and a covered passage or "tunnel" leading to the back between itself and the house next door. There were six steps up to Davis's front door, but the top one was a mere slab, making it more like five and a half steps. Inside the house there were a pair of brass candlesticks and a porcelain kingfisher on the piano, and upstairs there was a room with a large mirror over the fireplace and seven pictures, six of them views of mountains and the sea, as well as five large vases and two plaques that might well have been described as "funny saucers."

Everything was very much as "Gordon Davis" had told Dr. Soal, through the medium Blanche Cooper, back in January 1922. But Gordon Davis was not dead, and he and his wife and small son had not moved into the house described until about a year *after* the séance.

Absolute proof, signed and dated, is available of what was described at the séance in 1922 and of 54 Eastern Esplanade in 1925. The "voice" that spoke to Mrs. Cooper and Dr. Soal in 1922 was describing a place that *did not exist yet*, furnished as described, and yet was to exist in 1925. It was not the voice of Gordon Davis, for he was not *in* the spirit world (in fact, not even in the house) at that time.

HYPNOSIS HELPS

Professor Milan Ryzl taught a course at the University of California at San Diego in 1969 in which 150 students tried telepathy and clairvoyance both before and after being hypnotized. A control group of students who had not undergone hypnosis also tried the telepathic and clairvoyant experiments. Professor Ryzl claimed that hypnosis much increased psychic powers.

In Czechoslovakia, where he came from, he had asked his hypnotized psychics to give him numbers to play in the state lottery. There were forty-nine numbers on the card. His numbers were "good": he did not get the first prize (for that one had to guess six winning numbers) but he did receive a substantial prize for guessing four of the winning numbers. He attributed this to the psychics' help—and he spent his winnings on more laboratory equipment so he could continue to investigate their powers, before and after hypnosis.

Professor Thelma Moss of UCLA reports that some other university faculty are gambling successfully at Las Vegas, as a result of research.

WHAT WILL HAPPEN? SHALL I GET MY WISH?

European witches used orris root (*Iris florentina, Iris germanica, Iris pallida*) to give the answers to questions about the future. The root looks like a little crouching person; a thread was tied around the "neck" and held in the hand, so that the root dangled like a pendulum. Sitting alone at night, the questioner would pose the question and then concentrate. The pendulum would swing clockwise for "yes" and counterclockwise for "no," back and forth for "undecided."

This was a very popular version of coscinomancy (which involved two people balancing a suspended sieve) or cleidomancy (a key on the end of a string used as a pendulum). The pendulum is directed by unconscious or subconscious motions. It can be used over a map to locate treasure, water, and so forth, the pendulum substituting for a dowsing wand.

Experiment with a ring tied to a string and suspended into a glass. Can you *will* it to rotate in this direction or in that? Can you make it stop rotating once it has begun? Some people undoubtedly can move it, apparently at will. *Look Ma, no hands!*

WHERE THERE'S SMOKE, THERE'S LUCK

At Epiphany, celebrations in Tarcento, Italy, climax with a torchlight procession to the top of a nearby hill. This hill is not so famous as the Puy de Dôme in the Auvergne, France, where a temple of Mercury attracted medieval witches in droves, but it is known to have been the site of witchcraft in the past. So the moderns build their bonfire, tossing in their torches, and judge by the volume of smoke that comes from it whether the new year will bring prosperity or not.

REVELATIONS

One basic question people want answered is "When does the world end?" My answer—"when you die"—does not seem to satisfy.

As we have seen, the millenarians were sure the year 1000 was the date, whereas Nostradamus gives us a lot more time. Some people are getting ready for a Big Bang in 2000, and others are gathering on mountaintops to be whisked away at any moment.

In the 1960s, the authors of the musical *Hair* informed us that we were entering the Age of Aquarius, although any good astrologer could have told them differently, and in fact the hippies are not going to be around to enjoy it when it finally does arrive.

If you want a sounder prediction, try this one from a Benedictine monk of the last century, who wrote out a lot of them and sealed them in a lead tube. It was discovered, we are told, by Nicol Rycempel in Berlin when a church was demolished by bombs in 1944. The monk foretold a "trepidation of the spheres" in the eighties, perhaps a shift of the earth's axis "somewhere down the road" or the melting of the polar ice caps or . . . Well, I wouldn't worry about World War III, if I were you. A change of a couple of degrees in the earth's temperature could do a lot more damage to the world as we know it than any manmade catastrophe.

MICH THE WITCH

In an interview in *Playboy*, September 1981, novelist James A. Michener recalled an early period in his life when he was a professional fortune-teller for charity, calling himself Mich the Witch.

When I was in Egypt, I picked up a system of fortune-telling that was really quite extraordinary. I would answer *any* question specifically, in considerable detail. It was fraudulent from start to finish. But I would accidentally hit so close that it really became quite frightening.

There was one dramatic situation where I became sort of famous. This girl came in and the cards were such and such. I said, "How did the operation go?" She said, "What operation?" I said, "Your sex-change operation." Just out of the blue. And it was a guy in drag! It went all over the county. I got in the habit of saying the most outrageous things—and they were true. I got frightened by it. Once, I said, "Don't leave on the trip West Friday." And she left and a few miles from her home, her family was wiped out. When I was in Hawaii, I became very good friends with Henry Kaiser. He would come to have his fortune told. One day I said, "Henry, the banks are going to call your loan for $450,000,000, you'd better get things lined up." He went through the roof. "How did you know about this?!" What do you say to Henry Kaiser? You don't say ten bucks! I have a manuscript completed that will probably be published after I'm dead, about my experience in this. . . . It shows the roots of this mania and how it can be manipulated.

NEWS CONTROL

At Fátima in Portugal in 1917, three shepherd children reported having seen the Virgin Mary on six different occasions. The vision is said to have made certain prophecies concerning the end of the world. The information has been sealed, however, by officials of the Roman Catholic Church. The prophecies are supposed to be so startling that they caused Pope Pius XII to blanch when he read them.

In recent years, someone tried to hold hostages and compel the pope to release this information, but to no avail.

WHAT'S NEXT?

When, in the Babylonian epic of *Gilgamesh*, the hero asks his friend Enkidu how things are with the dead, Enkidu replies:

> I cannot tell it thee; if I were to open the earth before thee, if I were to tell thee that which I have seen, terror would overthrow thee, thou wouldst faint away.

Hamlet's father as a ghost in Shakespeare's play likewise refuses information about the afterlife:

> I could a tale unfold whose lightest word
> Would harrow up thy soul, freeze thy young blood,
> Make thy two eyes, like stars, start from their spheres,
> Thy knotted and combined locks to part,
> And each particular hair to stand on end,
> Like quills upon the fretful porpentine. . . .

Are you so sure, if you could look into the future, you would really want to know about What's Next?

BE OPTIMISTIC

If you suffer a reverse, try to think that in the future you will be glad about what happened. For instance, Napoleon applied for a job in the Russian army, but he didn't get it. He was holding out for the rank of major, and General Tamax thought the rank of captain was about as much as this obscure officer should expect. If Tamax's estimation had been higher, or Napoleon's demand lower . . .

A PRODIGY'S PREDICTION

Like Mozart, Christian Friedrich Heinecken started a brilliant career at the age of four. Few people have heard of "the Infant of Lübeck," however, because he did not live to establish a career, just to start it. He died in 1727 at the age of four, having predicted—in one or more of the several languages he spoke—his own death.

AND, FINALLY . . .

Maybe the best advice is that vouchsafed to historian Arnold Toynbee in a nightmare. He saw a Latin inscription that translates as "Hold on and pray."

7
Astrology

THE ZODIAC

There is no zodiac in the sky. The signs are merely human symbols for some of the celestial bodies we see from the earth. As the planets in their courses pass through the zones alloted to each of the zodiac figures, they are supposed to influence the course of life on earth.

KNOWLEDGE OF THE STARS

Astrology, they say, can give you knowledge of your character and your fate. People have believed that for thousands of years, so we know it *has* to be true, right? But I wonder about it, especially about those astrology columns in the newspapers. All the character delineations are so flattering, all the futures so rosy. Are they really writing and talking about us?

GLORIANA

Henry VIII countenanced strict laws against witchcraft but did not hesitate to consult astrologers about the sex of unborn children. They told him Elizabeth would be a boy. Even with a 50–50 chance, you can't win 'em all.

Elizabeth was luckier in her consultants and her reign (having chosen the date of her coronation with astrological advice). A few scholars allege her faithful John Dee also gave her the date of her death but was a little off. When the time came, she refused to lie down and stood for many hours, surrounded by her courtiers (who could not sit down if she would not), until she died—a little later than scheduled, perhaps, but (*semper eadem*) as determined as ever.

WATCH OUT FOR MARS

Many persons—among them President Theodore Roosevelt—have believed astrologers who warned them of the great dangers Mars can hold when that planet is in certain positions in the heavens.

Astrologers have been contending for many years that the planet to which we have given the name of the warlike god Mars exerts a baleful influence on men who are between the ages of forty-two and fifty-six and produces what has come to be called the midlife crisis.

Recent studies are beginning to clarify for many people the biorhythms, the swings of mood, the stages of mental development, the "passages" of significance in human lives, not just monthly peaks and troughs, not just rough bits in one's horoscope attributed to the actions or influence of Mars or any other planet.

AMERICA'S HOROSCOPE

Evangeline Adams (one of whose clients was Teddy Roosevelt) noted that the United States of America is a Cancer, born on July 4, 1776. She worked out a horoscope for the country. She predicted that the United States would get involved in World War II in 1942, and years later people found out she was twenty-two days off, because it was on December 8, 1941, that America declared war.

HOW OLD IS ASTROLOGY?

The foundation of the art or science of astrology (which, practitioners say, is like medicine, a little of both) may have been the doctrine of *quod superus est sicut quod inferus*, which is to say "as it is above, so it is below." This was the gist of the inscription on the Emerald Tablet said to have been found in the fist of Hermes Trismegistus, the "thrice-powerful" Egyptian god of alchemy and magic.

The study of the supposed influence of the stars above on human mundane affairs below used to be said to be the invention of the Chaldeans two or three thousand years before Christ (at whose birth some wise men, generally said to be three but most certainly astrologers, arrived, following the star to Bethlehem). Now it appears that the lore goes back to the Sumerians, some four thousand years before Christ.

But Serge Hutin in his learned *History of Astrology* (1970) contends that what is now popularly called astrology—individual predictions on the basis of the relative positions of heavenly bodies—was "a slow process, not appearing in fact before approximately 250 B.C." Those Magi were, in fact, students of a comparatively new science.

So astrology is both older and younger than its proponents generally claim. Since 250 B.C. there has been much devolopment of ceremonial astrology (foretelling the future with the aid of demons) and natal astrology (horoscopes). Perhaps the greatest astrologers were the Mayans. They said that time began in 3113 B.C. No sillier than Archbishop Ussher's calculation on the basis of the Bible that the earth was created in 4004 B.C., or just about the time that the Sumerians were inventing astrology.

STAR STATISTIC

In 1969, one documentary claimed, Americans spent $800 million on astrology. Today the figure may be well over $1 billion annually and growing.

DATE OF BIRTH

It is considered lucky to have the greatest distance possible between the number of your birth day and that of your birth month. Because of an odd way of calculating these numbers, (you add the second pair, so 27 = 9 and 31 is only 4), the best day of the year on which to be born is January 27. Mozart was born on that day. But January 18 would also give you a 1–9 relationship. Al Capone was born on January 18.

"JESUS CHRIST IS BORN TODAY. . . ."

The horoscope of Jesus Christ, wrote Ebenezer Sibley, shows a strong Libran influence.

I wonder if Mr. Sibley was working with the date December 25, which is just the date of the Saturnalia, taken over by the early Church to replace pagan celebrations with their own festivities. Christ could not have been born in late December if the sheperds were still "abiding in the fields" at the hour of his birth. His part of the country was too cold for that at that season of the year. Also, it turns out that Christ was born *before* the year from which we now calculate our *anno Domini*.

ACADEMIC FASHION

University professors tend to sneer at astrology, once part of the curriculum, but they may be interested to know that their academic gowns go back to the astrologers and students of black arts in twelfth-century Spain. Englishman Robert of Ketene studied at Toledo with Arabs and Jews and went to the University of Pamplona. Then he brought back to England much Arabic lore of astrology. He also brought the long Arab gown which became the familiar academic robe of Western universities.

ALL IN THE FAMILY, PART TWO

Ralph and Carolyn Cummins of Clintwood, Va., have produced five children. Catherine was born on February 20, 1952; Carol on February 20, 1953; Charles on February 20, 1956; Claudia on February 20, 1961; and Cecilia on February 20, 1966.

Something fishy about this? No, but they are all Pisces—just barely. Linda Goodman, author of the popular *Sun Signs*, says that their feet will be "noticeably small and dainty" or "they'll be huge and spread out like a washerwoman's." Their hands will be "tiny, fragile, and exquisitely formed— or else big ham bones that look as if they belong behind a plow." Something fishy about *that* kind of prediction, I think. . . .

RUINED BY A PREDICTION THAT WAS CORRECT

Richard James Morrison (1795–1874) published a number of extremely popular almanacs under the pen-name "Zadkiel." Morrison was ruined by what every astrologer strives for—a prediction that came true.

In 1861 "Zadkiel" announced that the year would see a serious health problem for Queen Victoria's beloved consort, Prince Albert. For a while it looked as if "Zadkiel" had goofed, but in December 1861 Prince Albert attended a function in cold and rain, came home and took to his bed, and died.

Morrison's stock sank to zero. No one likes bad news, even if well predicted.

"Zadkiel" continued until 1931, being taken over by Alfred James Pearce (1840–1923) and others who had better luck, as it were, than Mr. Morrison.

TIMING

People have always had ideas and superstitions about the best times for doing things. One of the earliest documents to be produced from movable type was a calendar, published at Mainz in 1462, which gave the astrological best times for bloodletting (then a very common treatment for unbalanced "humors," which were thought to be the cause of ill health). Of course, one of the most important times in a person's life is when he is born, hence the great emphasis that astrologers place on casting horoscopes for the exact moment a child takes its first breath.

KOHOUTEK

Remember the comet Kohoutek? In Saigon it was blamed for "the steeply rising price of rice, the shelling of Bien Hoa airport, and the imposition of Value Added Tax."

LIKE PARENTS, LIKE CHILD

Probably possessed of the highest I.Q. of anyone alive today, the young Korean genius Kim Ung-Yong (born 1963) may possibly owe some of his ability to the fact that his parents, both university professors, were both born at exactly the same time: 11 A.M. on May 23, 1934. He began talking at the age of five months and reading and writing at the age of seven months, but so far he has not spoken or written about this odd fact.

"THE FAULT, DEAR BRUTUS, LIES NOT IN OUR STARS. . . ."

The professor of agricultural economics at Aberdeen University announced in the 1970s that the 1975 business depression (recession, downward readjustment, panic, crisis—whatever you want to call such things) was due to a combination of heavenly influence and earthly uproar.

A book published some fifty years ago had the theory that sunspot activity, when combined with unusual volcanic activity on earth (filling our atmosphere with particles that blot out certain rays from the sun), adversely affects business cycles. Also, Commander David Williams (U.S.N., Ret.) in *Astro-Economics* (1969) argues that 68 percent of the major aspects of Jupiter, Saturn, and Uranus correlated with the bumpy ride of United States business graphs from 1761 to 1968. His theory of financial astrology was not new, and he admits that a clay tablet found in the ruins of Nineveh translates: "If Jupiter seems to enter the Moon, prices will be low in the country." The British economist W. Stanley Jevons in 1875 found correlations between sunspot activity and commodity price fluctuations. Commander Williams is bullish on America "until February 1992."

If you are interested in financial astrology, go into the market; there your theories will be no wilder than many others widely held. My advice (no charge) is buy cheaply something that inevitably must go up and then avoid mental activity concerned with money for a long while.

PARTRIDGE UP A TREE

Dean Jonathan Swift's satire *Predictions by Isaac Bickerstaff* stated flatly that the most popular astrologer of the day, John Partridge, would die on March 29, 1708. The day came and went, and on March 30, Swift published an account of the death. Mr. Partridge insisted he was still alive, but Swift and his friends blithely ignored that, and Partridge's "death" became a popular joke.

PAPAL ASTROLOGY

"How happy are the astrologers if they tell one truth to a hundred lies," wrote Francesco Guicciardini (1483–1540), a papal diplomat of great importance in the Renaissance, "while other people lose all credit if they tell one lie to a hundred truths."

In a time when most people were utterly convinced, however strong their orthodox faith, that the stars ruled human lives, even the popes relied heavily on astrologers. Julius II, Leo X, Sixtus IV, Adrian VI, and Paul III were just a few of those who would not make a move unless their stars dictated it. When the cardinals wanted Clement V, who had moved the papacy to Avignon, France, to return to Rome, they pointed out to him in astrological language that even the planets did best when in their own houses.

Jacques d'Euse, who reigned as John XXII (1313–1334), had not been able, even with the best astrological advice, to avoid a fatal disaster. He kept hale and hearty to the age of eighty-five despite difficulties all around him, but died when a ceiling fell on him. And the Renaissance popes were not always able to use a knowledge of the stars effectively against dangers that ranged from political intrigue to assassination attempts by witchcraft.

When anyone attacked their astrologers as heretics, as when Pope Honorius IV's physician and diviner Peter of Albano got into trouble in the late thirteenth century, the popes defended them briskly. Even Saint Thomas Aquinas admitted that "astrologers not infrequently forecast the truth by observing the stars" and attempted a pious explanation. Astrology began to be accepted almost universally. It was better than necromancy (which Albertus Grotius performed for Frederick Barbarossa) or the sort of thing that Archbishop Thomas à Becket got involved with to collect prophecies for his master, Henry II (palmistry and watching the flights of birds for auguries).

Then the powerful Council of Trent (1545–1563) ruled out astrological predictions, excepting only agriculture, navigation, and medicine. Sixtus V (pope 1572–85) issued a papal bull against the superstitious astrological charts, horoscopes, and predictions of his contemporaries—and, presumably, his own papal predecessors. The modern disapproval of astrology by the Catholic Church came into existence toward the end of the sixteenth century.

℞

I always thought the ℞ symbol at the head of a prescription was an abbreviation for *recipe*, the Latin for "take." Now I'm told some believe it doesn't mean *recipe* at all but is an "evolution of the astrological sign for Jupiter—an ancient invocation." Any pharmacists Out There ready to comment?

BAD BEGINNING

The horoscope cast for the Empress Maria Theresa's fifteenth child was so discouraging that the celebrations for the birth of the little girl were called off. The baby's name was Marie Antoinette.

KRAFFT ERRING

In World War II, Karl Ernst Krafft (1900–1945) was employed by the Nazis in the Ministry of Propaganda to cast horoscopes for both German and enemy personages. Hitler was a great believer in astrology. When Krafft tactlessly announced that the stars seemed much more favorable to Field Marshal Montgomery than to Field Marshal Rommel, Krafft's own future ceased to be bright. Krafft fell from power and eventually died in transit to the horror camp at Buchenwald; meanwhile the Desert War in North Africa had come out about as he had predicted.

YOUR SIGN

Depending on what time of day you were born on April 20, you're a Taurus or an Aries.

COLORFUL COMMENT

Avoid these colors: black (sorrow), purple (pride), yellow (lies), and orange (voluptuousness). Unless, of course, one is your lucky color.

Here is one of many lists that have been made of lucky colors:

Aquarius	(January 20–February 18)	Gray
Pisces	(February 19–March 20)	Blue
Aries	(March 21–April 20)	Red
Taurus	(April 21–May 20)	Dark green
Gemini	(May 21–June 20)	Brown
Cancer	(June 21–July 20)	Silver
Leo	(July 21–August 21)	Gold
Virgo	(August 22–September 22)	Orange
Libra	(September 23–October 22)	Pale green
Scorpio	(October 23–November 22)	Vermilion
Sagittarius	(November 23–December 20)	Sky blue
Capricorn	(December 21–January 19)	Black

In certain circumstances, these are unlucky colors: green (the fairies prefer it, and resent people using it), white (formerly a color of mourning), and red in your clothes or your hair (the first because *Leviticus* forbids the wearing of scarlet and the second because Judas Iscariot was supposed to have been a redhead).

On the other hand, green means hope, white means purity, and red means strength. Blue means trustworthiness and loyalty ("true blue"), rose goes with a gentle disposition, violet with intelligence, and purple with royalty. You may have to dress right to foretell the future.

Ecclesiastical vestments make use of symbolism in color that may have originally been connected to some belief in the "powers" of colors, and magical robes associate earth colors (green, russet), fire colors (scarlet, orange), water colors (blue) and yellow (for air) with the Four Elements, as well as assigning colors to the rituals that involve the planets, as follows: Sun (orange), Moon (violet), Mercury (yellow), Venus (green), Mars (scarlet), Jupiter (blue), Saturn (indigo).

"RAIN, RAIN, GO AWAY . . . ."

A Victorian ecclesiastic in his spare time figured out when Noah's Flood began. In case you're curious, it was November 25, 2348 B.C. It must have been a good thing; the planetary aspects that day were favorable.

PET THEORIES

After astrological cookbooks and such, it was only inevitable there would be a book about astrology and Fido. A few years ago a Los Angeles lady called Dorothy Macdonald obliged with *Astrology for Pets*. Pet-lover Cleveland Amory interviewed her for his syndicated column in 1975. He established with her that Cancer is a good sign for a pet ("very fluid") and that Gemini pets are "good companions, but they're restless." Mr. Amory produced this useful chart, which I reproduce from the May 22, 1975, *New York Post:*

If You Are	Best Pet	Worst Pet
Aries	Leo	Cancer, Scorpio
Taurus	Taurus, Virgo, Capricorn	Gemini, Libra, Aquarius
Gemini	Gemini, Libra, Aquarius	Virgo
Cancer	Cancer, Scorpio, Pisces	Aries, Libra
Leo	Leo, Sagittarius	Aries
Virgo	Taurus	Cancer, Sagittarius
Libra	Libra, Gemini	Aries, Cancer
Scorpio	Scorpio, Capricorn	Cancer
Sagittarius	Sagittarius, Aries, Leo	Pisces, Cancer
Capricorn	Taurus	Aries, Leo, Virgo
Aquarius	Gemini, Aries, Sagittarius	Leo
Pisces	Cancer, Taurus	Virgo

Miss Macdonald said she did not have to see the pet to cast the horoscope: "All I have to know is the approximate date of birth. I do them for horses too. For the next book, I'm going to do a goat."

THEY TOIL NOT, BUT THEY DO SPIN!

Charles IX was told by his astrologer that he could protect his life as many days as he could turn around, spinning on his heel, in an hour. So every morning Charles put in his hour spinning, in full sight of the principal officers of state, who (naturally) had to join in the spinning.

TELEVISION NONSTARS

Did you ever wonder why, with all the interest in astrology, there is nothing about it on television? Gary Marshall, creator of several very successful shows, says it's taboo. "The one absolute ban is anything to do with astrology," says *TV Guide*, and quotes Marshall (August 13, 1983):

Half the people in this country totally believe in astrology. The other half think its crazy. So either way, if it goes on television, it is sure to offend half the people in this country. No network wants that.

Meanwhile the consumers of pop culture who "totally believe in astrology" will have to make do with the many articles in those checkout-counter magazines they find in the supermarket, though the failure of their predictions, time after time, may be eroding their faith.

RAPHAEL THE ASTROLOGER

"Raphael" published almanacs for nearly a hundred years in England, down to the early 1930s. This is explained by the fact that several men wrote astrological predictions under this archangel's name. They included Robert Cross Smith (1795–1832) and Robert T. Cross (1850–1923).

FLOWER POWER

Each sign of the zodiac is associated with lucky or characteristic flowers. My sign (Sagittarius), for example, has pinks (the romantic side), dandelions (dislike of pretension—and lawnmowing), mosses (from the "rolling stone" aspect contradicted), and holly (prickliness, wariness). It makes a rather strange bouquet. What's yours?

PLACE OF BIRTH

Most people think only the day of the year they are born is astrologically significant but the time of day is important, too, and so is the place.

Robert and Deborah Brown were fans of the Texas Longhorns team and wanted their child to be born on Texas soil. But they lived in Oklahoma, so they got a bag of Texas soil and placed it under the delivery table at Mercy Hospital in Oklahoma City; there Deborah was born on October 4, 1978. How do you calculate *her* horoscope?

PLANET DAYS

In the lore of ancient astrologers, each day of the week had its ruling planet. After all these centuries, we still see evidence of this in these names of the days of the week: Sunday, Monday (Moon Day), and Saturday (Saturn's Day). Mars rules Tuesday (French *mardi*), Mercury rules Wednesday (though we call it after Woden), Jupiter rules Thursday (though our word stresses Thor), and Venus rules Friday (Freya's Day).

MORE ON LIFE CYCLES

Astrologers have long argued that the planets in their courses influence the ups and downs of our lives.

Jerome Cardan was described in *Transcendendal Magic* (first published in 1896) as "one of the boldest students, and beyond contradiction the most skilfull astrologer of his time." That time was the sixteenth century, a great age of astrology building on the work of Tommaso Pisano, Johann Regiomontanus, Johann Stöffler, and others, and featuring such outstanding personalities as Cosimo Ruggiero and Nostradamus. Cardan worked out cycles of 4, 8, 12, 19, and 30 years, based on the date of birth.

To ascertain the fortune of a given year, he sums up the events of those which have preceded it by 4, 8, 12, 19 and 30; the number 4 is that of Venus or natural things; 12 belongs to the cycle of Jupiter and corresponds to successes; 19 has reference to the cycles of the Moon and of Mars; the number 30 is that of Saturn or Fatality. Thus, for example, I desire to ascertain what will befall me in this present year. . . . I pass therefore in review those decisive events in the order of life and progress which occurred four years ago; the natural felicity or misfortune of eight years back; the successes or failures belonging to twelve years since; the vicissitudes and miseries or diseases which overtook me nineteen years [back] from now and my tragic or fatal experiences of thirty years back. . . .

I have left out some details because I do not recommend Cardan's system, but he has one extremely good idea. Before you worry about the future, why not sit down and review the past? Looking back on your life is always worth the effort. If you cannot learn from experience, how can you expect to be able to predict the future?

JANUARY 19 TO JANUARY 26

The "cusp" of Capricorn/Aquarius may be the best time for astrologers to be born, for persons born at this time have a flair for science—and also are "inclined to the fantastic and often support illogical ideas."

YOUR FATE IN THE CZARS

The Baronness von Krüdener, a mystic prominent at the court of Czar Alexander I (1777–1825), predicted both Napoleon's escape from Elba and his final fate. Alexander I was fascinated by such people, and one "Sister Salome" (Mme. Bouche) attended the czar from 1819 to 1821 and persuaded him to distribute solid gold talismans to defeat Napoleon.

On the other side Napoleon himself had some curious ideas; for instance, he dropped a *u* out of his last name so that it would be numerologically more potent.

When Alexander's brother succeeded him as Czar Nicholas I (1796–

1855) the influence of the occult continued. Nicholas depended much on the Polish mystic Hoene Wronski. His son Alexander II (1818–1881) put great faith in Baron Langsdorf's occult abilities. Among other things, the baron told him a bomb would explode at a dinner party in 1880 and persuaded the czar to arrive half an hour late. That saved his life. In 1881 the baron was sent on a mission to Paris; while the baron was away, the czar was killed by a bomb. That time he had no warning. His son Alexander III deeply believed that, had the baron only been present, his father's life would have been saved. Alexander III (1845–1894) had the baron consult the spirits every day via a sort of Ouija board and also was interested in astrological predictions. In 1886 the baron retired from "psychographic communication," due to failing health, and astrologers became more influential.

The last of the Romanovs, Czar Nicholas II, was a little less superstitious than his forebears but was intricately involved with mystics because his wife, the czarina, was completely in the power of the "mad monk" Rasputin. Rasputin knew nothing of astrology and cared nothing for Ouija boards, but his magnetic personality gave him remarkable powers. Among other things, he was the only person who could keep the czarevitch, Nicholas' son, from bleeding to death; hemophilia was a curse of the imperial family. The power of Rasputin ended with his sensational murder by Prince Yussoupov and others who had to poison him, bludgeon him, shoot him, and finally shove him through a hole in the ice-covered river, where at last he drowned. With Rasputin's demise the influence of occultists at court also more or less ended.

No wonder the czar did not see what was coming next.

No reliable evidence exists of any dependence by Lenin, Stalin, or more recent Russian rulers on seers, mediums, and astrologers. But the Soviets still want to know what the future holds. They are conducting scientific research in many branches of parapsychology. They are very interested in astrology, too.

ALL SETTLED

Genethlialogy is the "science" of casting horoscopes at birth, of predicting a person's entire life from the relations of the stars and planets at the exact moment he was born. But in these days when labor can be induced and the moment of birth to some extent controlled, I wonder if anyone undertakes to plan good constellations and a baby's time of arrival.

Perhaps the newspapers ought to give us information to help the unborn rather than the horoscopes they offer now. What is the best moment for conception? What is the best moment today and tomorrow for an infant to emerge? And now that the United States courts are going to have to deal with the problem of when that life actually *begins*, what effect will Congress have on American astrology and its—conceptions?

SCORPIO

If you look carefully, you may find astrological signs where you might not expect them. Charles, Prince of Wales, has a coronet of somewhat mod design that departs from tradition, and incorporated into the design is his sign of the zodiac, Scorpio.

Charles's personal horoscope may be the least favorable since that of William IV, but astrologers would say that a Scorpio is not at all a bad choice for a head of state. They also suggest he will not be able to look forward to taking over soon from Queen Elizabeth II, for no abdication is predicted in the near future, despite the fact that the pearls in her crown are supposed to be unlucky for a Taurus like her.

Theodore Roosevelt and Marie Antoinette were both Scorpios. So were Charles de Gaulle, Douglas MacArthur, and others who do not much seem to fit Linda Goodman's statement that "Scorpios love to travel incognito."

THE RULING PLANETS

In 1981 we entered the first Cycle of the Sun since the eighteenth century. The eighties will be governed as follows: 1981 Sun, 1982 Venus, 1983 Mercury, 1984 Moon, 1985 Saturn, 1986 Jupiter, 1987 Mars, 1988 Sun, 1989 Venus. Note that astrology is based on fewer planets than we now know actually exist, which ought to give us pause. The signs of the zodiac are twelve and run from March 21 through March 20 of the next year. I'm a Sagittarius (with Scorpio rising) with the same birth day as Otto Preminger and Walt Disney. Jupiter governs my sign, which is supposed to give me an exuberant, cheerful disposition. . . .

What about you?

8

Fortune-Telling

IN THE CARDS

Cards are probably the most common method by which fortunes are told these days. People use either Tarot or ordinary playing cards. Among the latter, the Ace of Hearts often signifies good news, the 9 victory. The Ace of Diamonds usually means a message or a document or a letter (favorable or unfavorable contents), the 9 of Diamonds advantage, the 7 good news. The Ace of Clubs is money, the 10 money, the 7 money. Stay away from Spades. The 9 of Spades is the worst card in the pack, but none of the Spades brings much hope.

INFERNO

In the Eighth Circle, near the bottom of Dante's Hell, the greatest Italian poet since Virgil puts usurers, simoniacs and scandalmongers, all sorts of hypocrites and thieves, even Odysseus and a pope (Nicholas III, reigned 1277–1280). Also joining that uncharmed circle are fortune-tellers, who wear their heads backward as a punishment for having tried to look forward too intently.

Dante himself actually engages in some prediction in this part of his poem. He has Pope Nicholas mistake him for Pope Boniface VIII (who did not die until 1303). Dante says that Boniface's arrival in Hell is expected any time, so Nicholas's error was understandable.

RITE ON!

There's hardly an alternative-lifestyle person anywhere these days who is not sitting around throwing the *I Ching* sticks, which the Chinese have given us along with gunpowder, paper, and tea.

Typically, the Chinese improved on something. Earlier people used coins or drew arrows at random from a quiver—like drawing straws. Belomancy (the arrow method) is now practically unknown, although we still draw straws in order to select a "volunteer." The improved Chinese system involved reading the cracks on heated bones or tortoise shells, but for accuracy it demanded real gifts of the reader. The modern *I Ching* comes with an instruction book, though even here some skill is required. Moreover, some latitude is permitted in interpretation, which means that (as with many ways of divining the future) your subconscious mind can come into play.

It could be that fortune-telling is not so much a way of talking to the fates as reaching your own inner self.

For centuries diviners have been trying to do one or both of these things by watching and reading the random way that sticks or cards or stones or tea leaves arrange themselves. The Tarahumares Indians of Mexico use human beings to perform this same kind of divination, called gyromancy. The Tarahumares, topped with wooden headdresses decorated with long streamers (and fueled with something a lot stronger than *yerba maté*), whirl around and around in their traditional dance until they collapse with exhaustion. Thereupon the tribal wisemen predict future events by the patterns formed by the fallen dancers.

Perhaps a combination of the *I Ching*, gyromancy, and rock 'n' roll music could be developed for the counterculture in America. Why not look at the way people "crashed" at a party? What does it tell you? Probably that you, as the only one who is still together, will have to clear up the pad after the love-in.

DICEY FUTURES

Since time immemorial dice have been thrown to tell fortunes. You start with a list of questions. Here is what people usually want to know:

1. Where does my future success lie?
2. Shall I be happy in love?
3. Am I in danger?
4. Will the action I propose succeed?
5. Will I find my lost article?
6. Will I get what I am asking for?
7. What should I now concentrate on?
8. Whom should I believe?
9. Should I change my job?
10. Am I loved by the person I love?
11. Shall I get involved in legal affairs?
12. Am I right to trust a certain person?
13. Shall I receive money owed to me?
14. What does the coming year hold for me?
15. Shall I hear from someone in whom I am interested?
16. Will my secret be discovered?
17. Should I travel?
18. Should I marry?
19. What does the immediate future hold for me?
20. Will he (or she) come back to me?
21. Where can I find happiness?
22. What are the most favorable times for action?
23. How can I get rich?
24. Shall I reach my goal?
25. Is something nice coming to me soon?

Along with this list must go a list of twenty-five responses for each possible combination of the dice. Suppose you throw a 4 and a 3. Consult the 4–3 list of replies. The 3–4 list is usually the same.

In dice games, 2–2 (craps) is not good. Here are the answers for 2–2 on the list provided for the system I am describing:

1. Wherever courage is required.
2. Yes, if your love is true.
3. Danger is always near, but never great.
4. Yes, if you start now.
5. In a hallway or among documents.
6. Eventually.
7. A personal matter such as illness, worry, revenge.
8. Someone whose reliability you trust.
9. Not for at least a few months.

10. Not now, maybe later.

11. Only if it is to your advantage.

12. They are okay except for a few minor details.

13. Don't expect more than part of it.

14. More money and bigger expenditures.

15. Not until your friend returns.

16. Not until it can do you little harm.

17. You will go sooner and more successfully than you have imagined.

18. After some hard times, marriage will turn out all right for you.

19. The answer you have long awaited.

20. When he or she is no longer wanted.

21. Outdoors.

22. Late autumn and early winter.

23. Stop wasting your money and time.

24. Probably, but too much indecision could prevent that.

25. You deserve it but someone is inconsiderate.

Walter and Litzka Gibson, in *Psychic Sciences*, and many others offer shorter or longer lists of questions and answers very like these for 2–2 and full lists of answers for the other dice combinations.

You can see that this requires a book in hand (or a terrific memory—the Gibsons give a list of questions and twenty-one lists of thirty answers in each case) and the replies are less manipulable and satisfactory than one gets simply by memorizing the "meanings" of the fifty-two cards in a pack.

Very few people throw dice any more to find out about their true love, and so forth. Some persist in throwing them to see if they can get rich. . . .

YES AND NO

Does the Ouija board work? Well, yes and no. But it is called Ouija from the French for "yes" and the German for "yes." It is *not* some ancient cabalistic device but a commercial product first patented in 1892 by a Maryland novelty company.

DREAM BOOKS

Many people are devoted to "dream books," which list all the "meanings" of the symbols and situations that crop up in dreams. Psychoanalysts are interested in your dreams, too, but not in oneiromancy (fortune-telling through dreams). *All* your dreams make them rich.

Still the best "dream book" may be that of Artemidorus Daldianus, second-century soothsayer, whose multivolume dictionary of dreams was criticized for offering such latitude that a dream could be interpreted to mean just about anything you wanted it to mean. Or you can check the syndicated column on the interpretation of dreams that runs in hundreds of American newspapers, which is more specific. Or your gypsy handbook. Or even the works of such modern greats as Carl Jung, who concluded that in dreams we use our past and plan our future and get in touch with all that is stored in the attic of our mind.

CRYSTAL BALL

The ancient Jews practiced scrying with bowls of water, but you can use a black mirror, a glass ball, an ink blob, or a real ball of crystal (preferably with a slightly bluish tinge). Any one of them will concentrate the mind. I know one seer who has obtained striking results by staring into the screen of her television set when the set is turned off.

Actually, if you will concentrate on *any* object, you will find that you can summon powers of the mind that you use all too infrequently and may be able to bring to the surface insights and intuitions that will amaze you. Try it.

AUTOMATIC WRITING

Mediums in trance have been able to write, often at incredible speeds, messages "dictated from beyond the grave." One of the most amazing was Mrs. Verrall, who could "transmit" in automatic writing vast quantities of Latin and Greek, languages that she said she did not know. (Of course her husband was a professor of classical languages.)

Others see automatic writing as a way of getting into touch with the subconscious, which may be Another Life just as astounding as that of the Beyond.

Some of William Butler Yeats's poetry was the result of automatic writing. Alfred, Lord Tennyson also used to write in a state of trance. But the results of most automatic writing experiences are less impressive.

GYPSY QUEEN

Everyone was wrong about the origin of gypsies. Their name in English suggests they came from Egypt. Others thought they came from Bohemia, hence *bohemians* for unconventional people. Or even Flanders, hence the Spanish *flamencos*. Today they are believed to have originated in India. In any event, the Romany-speaking people wandered all over Europe, spreading the ancient arts of fortune-telling.

My favorite gypsy fortune-teller in history is Margaret Finch (1631–1740). She lived to be 108, for one thing. For another, she was the gypsy queen of Norwood in Kent, England. Even more striking, for the last forty years of her long life, she crouched on the ground so much that she could not straighten up and had to move from place to place in a sitting waddle. When she finally died, they buried her with her knees still bent, in a square coffin.

ANCIENT ORACLE

Everybody knows about the oracle at Delphi and other marvels of the classical world, but have you heard of the Hypogeum or underground temple of Hal Suflitti (dating from 3000 B.C.) discovered on Malta in 1902? It was found to contain 33,000 human bones and a hole through which the oracle could speak. If those dry bones could speak, what a story they would have to tell!

"ART THERE, OLD MOLE. . . ?"

A mole on the right side of the forehead was thought to indicate talent and promise success. A mole on the left side? You are stubborn, extravagant, dissolute. A mole on the right hand? Money will come to you. A mole on the left hand? Sensitivity and artistic ability.

FATHER BROWN'S OPINION

"If a fortune-teller trades in truth," said G. K. Chesterton's famous detective-priest, Father Brown, "then I think he is trading with the enemy."

HANDS UP!

The ancient art of palmistry would take one or more books just in itself. But look at the nail joint of your thumb. If it is especially bulbous, you are or will be a murderer. A very short little finger indicates mental deficiency, and a long one bodes well for academic success. If your life line shows breaks or splits, move. If your head line terminates under Saturn and your life line shows weakness, expect premature death. If you have the same weak head line, but your life line is stronger, you will just go insane, not die young.

And if you don't know your head line from your life line, why not find an illustrated book on palmistry and give it the once-over as to chirognomy (the general shape and formation of the hand, fingers, and thumb) and chirosophy (the significance of the lines, bumps, etc.)? You may find there some information on whether you have psychic abilities.

Try this. Put your left hand on the table, palm up. The lower right side of your palm has a bump dedicated to the Moon (Luna). Your little finger is dedicated to Mercury. (You see that palmistry and astrology are connected, but we won't get into that, just the names.) You may find a Line of Intuition extending like a crescent from the lowest part of the Mount of Luna to the line that runs up to your little finger, the Area of Mercury. The bend of the crescent should be inward, toward the center of your palm; if it bends the other way, you may have many premonitions and hunches, but they will mostly be wrong. A solid line formation indicates good psychic abilities. If you have similar lines in both hands, you may devote yourself to the occult. If your line of intuition is under your middle (Saturn) finger with a cross, you combine the religious with the occult. If your line of intuition terminates in the upper part of the central palm (Plain of Mars), you have hypnotic powers or at least a charismatic personality. If there is an "island" formed by two lines diverging and then coming together again near the beginning of your line of intuition, you may walk in your sleep. Keep your head line away from your line of intuition if you can. If it crosses it, you'll go at least temporarily insane. If that already obtains and your thumb is small and your hand generally weak, you are probably incurably crazy already.

But this is too difficult to follow, and a hand must be examined in all its aspects. The classic of chiromancy and related arts (or sciences) is *Cheiro's Language of the Hand*. "Cheiro" is the pseudonym for a man who was for many years the leading authority on chiromancy and wrote about palmistry in general while serving also as a reporter, war correspondent, and newspaper editor.

Once Mark Twain went to him to have his hands read. "The one humorous point in the situation is," Mr. Clemens told Cheiro, "that I came here expecting to lose my money by my foolishness, but I have gained a plot for a story which I certainly think should be a 'best-seller.'"

The story became *Pudd'n Head Wilson*. The plot hinges on thumb prints. The famous American author wrote in the London seer's visitor's book; "'Cheiro' has exposed my character to me with humiliating accuracy. I ought not to confess this accuracy, still I am moved to do it."

YOUR CHOICE, YOUR FUTURE

In *Occultism*, expert Julien Tondriau lists more than a hundred ways of fortune-telling and prediction. The nastiest I can think of was tried by Manasseh, king of Judah, 692–638 B.C. He used to tell the future by tearing open young boys and examining the guts. It's called anthropomancy, and worse. The terrible Gilles de Rais in the Middle Ages also practised anthropomancy and murdered hundreds of boys to do it.

SO YOU NEVER WERE ANY GOOD AT MATH?

Mary Russell Mitford (1787–1855), English novelist, at the age of ten dreamed of the number 7 on three successive nights. So she multiplied 7 by 3; and bought a lottery ticket with the number 22. Her arithmetic may have been no good, but her luck was tremendous. She won the equivalent of about $150,000 or $200,000. Of course, had she known her multiplication tables better she would have put her money on 21 and won nothing. There's a moral in this somewhere.

SUITED TO A TEA

For tasseography or teacup reading, use a genuine teacup—that is, a plain cup with slanted sides or one resembling a bowl. (Teacups were first bowls anyway, without handles, as Oriental cups still are.) Drink most of your tea, invert the cup on the saucer, and with your left hand turn the cup around on the saucer three times left to right. There will be some leaves on the bottom of the cup, some on the sides, some near the rim. Those on the bottom indicate the distant future, those near the rim the immediate future. You read with the cup in your left hand, holding the handle, and from the handle to the left and around, getting more and more into the future as you go. The tea stems, if any, represent men and women, respectively long and short.

As to the meaning of the shapes you see, you will need a guidebook or a lot of intuition.

ALL ABOARD!

Jerome Cardan, sixteenth-century astrologer, named the lines on people's foreheads for the various planets known in his time. Hairline to eyebrows in order downward, they were Saturn, Jupiter, Mars, Sun, Venus, Mercury, Moon. Cardan also ascribed attributes to them associated with astrological beliefs. Wavy lines suggested travel by sea, but lines that turned up at the end (travel by air) he had to ignore, since there was no method of flying then available.

The authors of *Psychic Sciences* write: "Today, an airline passenger will do well to note the forehead lines of other persons on the plane. It may be surprising to learn how many turn up at the ends."

I have been watching the corners of the mouths of railway passengers. They tend to turn down, which often indicates that the train is running late.

FIRST STEPS

William Woods's *History of the Devil* (1973) contains these assertions about clairvoyance (clear vision into the future) and precognition (knowing what is going to happen):

The Marquise du Deffand, having been told that St. Denis walked two leagues, carrying his head in his hands, is said to have replied, *"La distance n'y fait rien; il n'y a que le premier pas qui coûte."* [The distance doesn't matter; it's only the first step that counts.] If [university researcher in parapsychology] Rhine can demonstrate, as he has beyond question, that certain individuals are consistently precognitive, that they can foretell, sometimes against odds of hundreds of thousands to one, the sequence in which certain cards will fall, and that they can do this over and over again, then the case is proved. It does not matter that only one in a thousand can do this. *C'est le premier pas qui coûte.* We may lack the power ourselves, but clairvoyance and precognition exist.

Call it intuitive perception, call it an illogical but consistently accurate leap into the dark, or acuity in the analysis of otherwise imperceptible evidence, or a higher gear in the power of logical reasoning, certain people have always claimed to possess it and most of us have at least superficial evidence that it exists. . . . We simply have to admit that these things happen and that scientific causality has so far been inadequate to explain them. We do not understand. Perhaps we have forgotten even more than we have learned.

A SCIENCE WITH BOTH FEET ON THE GROUND

The Chinese not only read palms, they read feet (podoscopy).

WHICH WITCH?

With a prescription in Exodus not to suffer a witch to live, how could Saul consult the witch of Endor (I Samuel)? Because she was not a witch at all; she was a diviner. Still she was dabbling in forbidden arts, and Saul could only get her to raise the spirit of Samuel for him by promising not to betray her.

THE TAROT

All sorts of people from the barber Alliette to "The Beast" Crowley, from Lord Alfred Douglas to Eden Gray, Bill Butler, "MacGregor" Mathers, Mayananda, "Papus," A. E. Waite, Paul Foster Case, to Arland Ussher and "Eliphas Lévi" have written extensively on the Tarot cards. These fortune-telling cards are sometimes said to have derived from ancient Egyptian mysteries but actually were invented in the late twelfth or early thirteenth century. Playing cards were first banned by Alfonso XI, King of Leon and Castile, in 1332, but the court accounts of Charles VI, King of France, 1392, mention payment for three sets of the Tarot arcana. That French king was insane and superstitious.

The Tarot deck consists of two kinds of cards. First are "minor arcana," resembling our modern playing cards, with four suits, each of ten cards (1–10) and four "face cards" (Page, Knight, Queen, King), as follows:

Pentacles (or Coins) corresponding to our Diamonds.
Wands (or Batons) corresponding to our Clubs.
Cups (or Chalices) corresponding to our Hearts.
Swords (or Epées) corresponding to our Spades.

Then there is a "major arcana" of cards, bearing ancient and much-debated symbols (now twenty-two). So the whole pack consists of seventy-eight cards. Most beginners work only with the major arcana. The minor arcana, ranked Pentacles, Wands, Cups, Swords, the last being highest (as our slang term "in spades" suggests), involve far longer and more complicated procedures for fortune-telling than the major. In recent times, however, people have seemed to seek even larger decks (such as the Morgan deck of eighty-seven cards) and more complexity as well as shorter decks (the Jesus Deck and George Muchery's Astrological Deck each contain only forty-eight cards). The Gypsy Method uses the Fool as "significator" and the twenty-one other major arcana only, while a Planetary Arrangement uses all seventy-eight in *I Ching* trigrams of Fu Hsi. The Churchyard Spread takes out the Fool card, shuffles the remaining seventy-seven, counts out twelve, adds the Fool, and shuffles, and works with thirteen. Mathers's long method in *The Tarot* (1888) uses all the cards and an almost interminable amount of time to run through eleven separate stages of "reading."

I'll spare you a description of that, remarking that fortune-telling by the Tarot is only tangentially related to magic or witchcraft, being neither itself. It is, in fact, only a system for getting into your subconscious. Bill Butler's eminently sensible *The Definitive Tarot* (1975) begins this way:

The cards are not magic. They do not tell the future, they cannot evaluate the past. In the hands of a skilled practitioner they can be used in two different ways for the study of the unconscious mind. The first is for a reader to relate the symbology of the cards as they "fall" in a reading . . . adding as little personal interpretation as possible. The evaluation is performed by the Querent, to whom the question is real and known and the answer is made manifest through the reader . . . [who can be] a relatively unskilled reader.

In the second method the reader, a skilled clairvoyant, uses the Tarot as a vehicle for concentration, a sort of patterned mirror reflecting to an inner eye the features of a landscape in someone else's mind. Both methods rely on the Querent to provide the answer, on the theory that some shadow of events to come is thrown across the unconscious days and perhaps years before the eruption of physical event. As shadows by their nature are not "fixed" it seems likely that shadows of the future are no more fixed. . . .

The Tarot can tell, not compell; it deals in possibilities, not fates. What has not happened need not happen; with knowledge from the Tarot, the questioner may alter the course of the future described. The Tarot simply taps the unconscious. The rule is the same as with computers: "garbage in, garbage out."

To hint at the complexity of dealing with the information stimulated by the symbols on the cards, let us look at one of the most famous, the Hanged Man. Waite suggests this card is full of significance, all veiled, but relates it to willing sacrifice, circumspection, intuition, divination, prophecy.

Magicians will note in the Hanged Man, the twelfth card of the major arcana, a sacrifice to Odin hanging on Yggdrasil (Odin's ash tree), and think of the Hand of Glory, the magical touch of a hanged man's hand, gallows' sweat, and other weird ingredients of ointments, the relation to the Great Work and the turning point in the psychic life, the ambiguity of the lamed but gifted one, etc., bound by Fate but never in pain.

Astrologers will emphasize Neptune (as Case, Crowley, and some others do), Mars acting on Mercury (the Golden Dawn), Scorpio (Mayananda), Libra (Ussher and "Papus"), Pisces (A. E. Thierens), etc. Considerable disagreement here.

Butler gives pages of different interpretations by almost twenty authorities, and he himself in his Introduction says of the "Magician/Fool/Devil/Hierophant/Hermit/Hanged Man," naming some major symbols of the deck, that whatever you call him "he is Hermes, he is Thoth." Grimaud plays down the importance of the Hanged Man; others think him crucial (no pun intended). Many stress that he is always shown in no pain, while Crowley sees "enforced sacrifice, punishment, loss, fatal and not voluntary, suffering." Clearly, one reflects one's own personality in "reading" this or any other card. I see joyous sacrifice, renunciation leading to revelation, transition to triumph, surrender to enlightenment. Even in the Chariot, along with war, vengeance, and trouble, I see victory, equilibrium, solution, and as the seventh card I cannot deem the Chariot very unlucky. Now the thirteenth, Death, is another matter; the best that even an optimist can see there is "sudden change."

What do you see?

Remember, if you will, what eighteenth-century German satirist Georg Lichtenberg said of a mirror: If a monkey looks into it, you cannot expect an angel to look out.

But if you are ready to look into yourself and face what you find, the Tarot is there, not as something magical, but just as a mirror of innermost thoughts, feelings, insights, intuitions.

Here is the shortest explanation I can make of a simple reading. Take the twenty-two cards of the major arcana and place the Fool as "significator" right side up in front of the Questioner (seated opposite the Reader). Place the rest of the cards in numerical order, all right end up (top at the top):

I The Magician/Juggler	XII The Hanged Man
II The High Priestess	XIII Death
III The Empress	XIV Temperance
IV The Emperor	XV The Devil
V The Heirophant/Pope	XVI The House of God/
VI The Lovers	Tower Struck by Lightning
VII The Chariot	XVII The Star
VIII Justice	XVIII The Moon
IX The Hermit	XIX The Sun
X The Wheel of Fortune	XX Judgment
XI Strength	XXI The World

The Questioner, emptying his or her mind of all other thoughts or desires except the question to be silently asked, shuffles the cards face down as much as desired and places the pack face down in front of the Reader. The Reader cuts the cards three times with the left hand to the left and reassembles the pack.

The Reader then deals the cards, all of them to be viewed from the point of view of the Questioner (cards upside down are read as weakened or even reversed, and cards influence the reading of those near them), as follows:

> One card in the center of the table (Present Influence).
> One card across that left to right (Immediate Obstacles).
> One card above that (Goal of the Present Question).
> One card below (Past Foundations of the Current Situation).
> One card to the right of the two crossed in the center (Past Foundations).
> One card to the left of the two crossed in the center (Future Influences).
> Four cards above the other, bottom to top on the right of all the cards previously laid out; these represent respectively (from bottom to top) the Questioner, the Environment of the Questioner, the Questioner's Inner Feelings or Thoughts, the Final Result of all the other cards.

The Reader interprets and relates the cards in relation to the question (which ought never to be spoken). You may not read your own fortune, ever. I know some people disagree with that, but they are wrong.

IT DEPENDS ON HOW YOU LOOK AT IT

The Greek augurs faced north for divining the future; signs on the east, at their right hand, were regarded as favorable. The Roman augurs faced south when operating, which put favorable signs in the west, on their right hands. Those in the east, at the left, were *sinister*.

FORTUNA

The Romans worshipped a goddess called Fortuna (Fortune), who had previously been a harvest deity and who therefore continued to be shown with a cornucopia of abundance. In her temple at Praeneste, Fortuna told fortunes with a pile of wooden tiles on which messages had been written; a child pulled out a tile at random, and the message was interpreted for the questioner. The same sort of thing goes on in the streets of big cities today where, for instance, a trained bird will pick a little piece of paper with your "fortune" on it from a collection placed in his trainer's tray.

A sobering thought: The Romans often portrayed Fortuna standing on a ball, not to show that she dominates the world but to suggest the instability of luck.

DEWEY-EYED INNOCENCE

American presidential elections are famous for their irrational qualities, but the unsuccessful campaign of Thomas E. Dewey in 1948 set some kind of record. For one thing, the *Chicago Tribune* jumped the gun and headlined its election story "Dewey Wins." For another, the candidate himself came up with a classic pronouncement: "You know that your future is still ahead of you."

May your future be full of what we turn to next—luck.

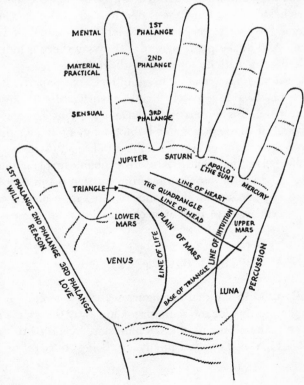

9
Luck

PICK A NUMBER

When asked to pick a number (between 1 and 10 or some such), more people will choose an odd number than an even. "Why do we all believe that odd numbers are best?" asked Pliny the Elder. Actually, Virgil had answered that question some forty years earlier in his Eighth Eclogue: "God delights in odd numbers." And Shakespeare agreed; "They say there is a divinity in odd numbers, either in nativity, chance or death."

Many superstitions are related to numbers, particularly 3 and 7. Consider the ban on three to a match. British investigators, trying to track down the antiquity of this superstition, have gotten as far back as the Crimean War, when, if you kept a match lighted long enough for three men to use it, you were giving the enemy something to fire at. (Matches don't go back much farther than the 1850s.) A more probable explanation is that British soldiers picked up the superstition from Russian prisoners of war. In Russia, altar candles were lighted in batches of three from one taper, and it was considered sacrilegious to light nonreligious items in threes.

SUPERSTITIOUS SCULPTOR

Michelangelo used to say that the figure was there already inside the block of marble just waiting for the sculptor to chip away the excess material imprisoning it; he spoke of freeing the sleeping statue. The British sculptor John Deare (1758–1798) had another theory. He believed that if he slept on

132

top of a block of marble he would awake inspired to create masterpieces like Michelangelo's. All that happened is that he slept on some cold marble, caught a bad cold, and died.

8

The Chinese considered 8 a very lucky number. One Chinese in Hong Kong paid £2800 for the right to the car license number 8888.

TAKING A CHANCE

They cast lots to see who would take on Hector, how the Promised Land would be divvied up, to select the scapegoat of the Jews, to obtain possession of the garment Christ discarded at the foot of the Cross.

Jonah wound up in the belly of the whale because the sailors, terrified of a violent storm, cast lots to see who was the cause of it, and the choice fell on Jonah. He was thrown overboard to appease the Lord.

Out of lots came lotteries (which Voltaire rightly called "a tax on ignorance" but which give much hope to millions). One duke of Burgundy tried to recoup his losses to Italian bankers by taking a cut of lotteries, the king of France tried to finance bridges and wars by lotteries, Elizabeth I of England started a lottery to repair her ports (1566), and over the centuries rich and poor alike have had a "flyer" and hoped to repair their fortunes with One Big Win on something like a state lottery or the Irish Sweepstakes or the Mexican or Canadian lotteries, and so on.

That same Voltaire referred to a vapid portrait of the assembled ruling family of Spain as seeming to show "a butcher who had just won the National Lottery." Some nobodies did get really rich.

Ernie Eban in the *Village Voice* (June 26, 1978), in an entertaining survey of the lottery craze over the centuries, touches on something related to charms and spells when he notes that in Elizabethan England ticket buyers were identified not by name or number but by posies, brief verses they wrote on their tickets. Thus:

> "I am a pore maiden
> and fain would marry

And the lack of goods
is the cause I tarry"
or
"I was begotten in Calice [Calais] and born in Kent
God send me a good lot to pay my rent."

Then the buyers had to wait thirteen years until enough tickets were sold to justify distribution of the prizes. Today the results are on TV pretty quickly.

FRIDAY THE THIRTEENTH

When you put together the day of the Crucifixion and the number of Christ and the apostles (with the traitor Judas Iscariot included) you get a date which even some people who claim not to be superstitious at all find very uncomfortable. Ripley once constructed a remarkable list, however, of Fridays the thirteenth to show how lucky a date it was in American history.

Believe it or not, the thirteenth of the month falls on Friday more often than on any other day. Take a period of four hundred years, longer than you are going to have to worry about but a basic unit of the calendar, and you will find that, over that period, there will be 688 Fridays the thirteenth. Of Sundays and Wednesdays, the next most recurrent thirteenths, there will be 687.

MORE THIRTEENS

On the Great Seal of the United States there are thirteen stars, thirteen stripes, an eagle with thirteen feathers in each wing and thirteen feathers in its tail (it holds in one claw thirteen arrows and in the other a laurel branch with thirteen leaves and thirteen berries), thirteen letters in the motto beneath, thirteen clouds in the glory above. This is THE COAT OF ARMS OF THE UNITED STATES OF AMERICA. Count the letters—39, or 13 times 3. Which must make this the most unsuperstitious heraldic device in the world—no triskaidekaphobia here.

MONDAY NEED NOT BE BLUE

You will have good luck all week if you get pennies in change on a Monday. If you get one with the date of your birth on it, keep it for extra luck. The best thing is to find a penny with that date on it. But finding any kind of money is undoubtedly lucky.

OFF ON THE RIGHT FOOT

Britain's new National Theatre was opened in March 1976. That was the culmination of 128 years of bandying about the concept. Both houses of Parliament passed the necessary legislation without a division decades before, but still the project languished. Denys Lansdun, the architect, designed an aggressively ultramodern concrete monster in the Brutalist style and lived to see his design grow old-fashioned before it was built, for it took twelve years from drawing board to £16 million reality. There was only one piece of real stone in the concrete mass, the cornerstone—and that was one of four laid in different places at various times. It had been laid in 1951, on another site.

At the last minute the long-awaited building was not opened to the public on the date announced. It was not because the building was unfinished—they decided to open with only one of the three theaters in the building ready to go—but because someone pointed out that the chosen opening date was unlucky. It was the Ides of March.

RESULTS OF DOING UNLUCKY THINGS

American folklore says these results are to be expected if you ignorantly or foolishly do the following:

If you sneeze at the table,	a death in the family.
If you hear a dove mourn as the New Year breaks and you happen to be going downhill at the time,	bad luck for the coming year.
If you break a mirror,	seven years bad luck.

If you kill a frog,	the cow will die.
If you trim your nails on a Sunday,	you will fall sick by next Sunday.
If you sweep trash out the cabin door at night,	the slaveowner will sell you.
If you count graves,	bad luck.
If you drop a book and fail to step on it,	worse luck.
If he proposes to you in church,	the marriage will be unlucky.
Sneeze on Sunday,	Hell all the week.

JUST LUCKY?

"Some people have all the luck," you hear people say. But it could be that most people really make their own luck. As Benjamin Disraeli said, "We make our destinies and call them fate," and for some "luck" is actually careful foresight or the ability to take advantage of what comes along.

One man who made his own good fortune was architect Ranulf Flambard. He built the Tower of London and then was unlucky enough to be the first man to be imprisoned in that stout fortress. But he escaped, because as the architect, he knew a secret way out.

A LAMP UNTO MY FEET

Lamps shaped like a human foot were exchanged by the ancient Romans as a New Year gift. The belief was that they would prevent missteps in the coming year. (Romans were very superstitious and almost all their children wore amulets.)

COINCIDENCES

Coincidence is one of the most prolific origins of superstition. When a string of coincidences happens, people tend to seek far-out explanations, just as their judgment is affected by the coin that turns up heads ten times in a row. Actually the odds that it will turn up heads on the eleventh toss are still 50–50, but try to convince people of that. If you think of someone and the next instant the phone rings, that's odd. Is it any odder if this happens with ten phone calls in one day?

A lot of so-called magic is intricately tied up with coincidence, and there's nothing magical about it at all. But people have been willing to believe the strangest things.

For a remarkable string of coincidences, try this: Maximilian Joseph (1756–1825), king of Bavaria, celebrated not his actual birthday but the feast day of his patron saint, which fell on October 12. In the last six years of his reign there was no official celebration on that day. On October 12, 1820, the royal palace burned down. On October 12, 1821, his favorite servant died. On October 12, 1822, one of his ministers lost a hand in an explosion. On October 12, 1823, the queen suffered a severe hemorrhage. On October 12, 1824, several workmen were killed when a wall of the palace collapsed. On October 12, 1825, (or, perhaps, October 13) the king died.

Some people would say October 12 was Max Joseph's unlucky day, even that some kind of curse was put on it. What is your opinion?

LUCKY AT DOWSING

In the first half of this century, the Government of India hired Major C. A. Pogson as water diviner. In his three years of searching for water with the traditional forked stick, he chalked up a record of 93 percent accuracy.

You can even hold your dowsing or divining rod (preferably of hazel) over a map and find water, mines, buried treasure, and so on, by what is called radiesthesia, but some parapsychological powers, if not incantations, are said to be necessary to success. Not everyone can do it, and few can compete with the "gifted" diviners such as Major Pogson.

A MINISTERING ANGEL, THOU

Some people are lucky enough, they say, to get help from angels—not the theatrical kind, but the supernatural. Handel claimed he had seen the whole host of heaven before him when he dashed off the "Hallelujah Chorus" of *The Messiah*, a composition so stirring that it even got King George II to his feet (which is why audiences today traditionally stand for that particular chorus). Confined to a sanitorium during the final two years of his life, the composer Schumann made a similar astounding claim. He was lucky enough to have angels dictating music to him. Blake said an archangel appeared to him and taught him how to draw. Poet Allen Ginsberg claims Blake once appeared to him when he was a young student at Columbia University, but Ginsberg claims the figure was wearing "a toga," so it probably wasn't Blake at all.

BAD LUCK DEATHS

Fabius, "the Roman praetor," drank a glass of goat's milk containing one goat hair. He choked and died. The only English pope, Nicholas Breakspear, who reigned from 1154 to 1159 as Adrian IV, got into a tizzy cursing the Emperor Frederick I, took a drink from a fountain to refresh himself, choked on a fly, and died. William III (of Britain) died as a result of an accident: his horse tripped on a molehill. Clive of India (1725–1774) aimed a pistol at his own head and twice pulled the trigger. The pistol did not go off. When he asked his friend Maskelyne to come into the room and fire the pistol out the window, it did fire. "Well, I must be reserved for something," said Clive and went on to establish the British *raj* in India. Years later, he tried suicide again, because he thought his work was done and he was ill. The pistol fired without a hitch. Guy de Maupassant (1850–1893), in the last stages of syphilis, suffered many delusions (including the idea that his brain was leaking out through his nose) and cut his throat; they stitched him up and put him in a "sanitorium" in Paris, where he lived more than a year more. When Gamal Abdul Nasser (1918–1970) was a child he read in the Koran that anyone who died before the age of seven would not go to hell, so when he was six he attempted suicide by eating sealing wax.

THE VISIONS OF BLAISE PASCAL

He had something of a wild youth, or as wild a one as was consistent with devoting himself to mathematics, working out the geometrical theorems of Euclid independently for himself, and inventing the adding machine before he reached the age of ten. At about thirty Blaise Pascal underwent a religious conversion that suddenly made him an ascetic, a recluse, and a visionary. The last quarter of his life was spent in its shadow.

He moved into a sparsely furnished room and enjoyed no comforts he could do without, ignoring the servants of his wealthy household and taking care of himself in the simplest way. He spent most of his waking hours in prayer, reading the Bible, and writing down pious thoughts (*pensées*). He hardly ate.

He imagined that a yawning abyss opened up on one side of him wherever he went and "would never sit down till a chair was placed there to secure him from apprehended danger." He committed to paper another vision that he was unlucky (or lucky?) enough to have and then sewed the document into his coat lining so that it would accompany him everywhere he went. What was on the paper was a secret, and one that seems to have died with him.

An Italian mathematician of note, Jerome Cardan (the English form of his name), was convinced he was accompanied everywhere by "an aerial spirit, partly emanated from Saturn, and partly from Mercury." Cardan had delved deeply into the cabala and even black magic, but Pascal simply was "born again" and had a traumatic religious experience, a watershed vision of God in his life. Pascal did not have to turn to magic for happenings or hallucinations. Just reading the Scripture produced the most moving and terrifying visions for him. Some saints and many ordinary people have reported a great joy in religious ecstasy; others have felt a sense of being consumed in fire or a loss of self in ecstatic union with the eternal. But Pascal's vision was frightening, as crippling as Swedenborg's famous "fear and trembling." It haunted and darkened his life. Was it madness, or something even less understood?

HORSESHOES

People hang horseshoes up over a door for good luck but too few know that the superstition requires the shoes be nailed up with the ends upward. Otherwise "good luck drains out of the ends."

LUCKY 7

If your lucky number is 7 (and not everybody's is), not only is the seventh day of the month a propitious one for you, but so are the numbers that add up to 7. Expect good luck also on the sixteenth and the twenty-fifth.

RELIABLE SUPPORT

On February 23, 1895, John Lee mounted the scaffold in Exeter, England. He had been condemned to be hanged. They tried, but four times the trapdoor failed to open when the hangman threw the lever, though each time it had been inspected and tested and had worked fine. When the governor of the prison stood on it himself, sure it would stick again, it opened, and he fell through.

After four attempts to hang John Lee, prison officials gave up and consulted the Home Secretary. He granted a stay of execution and later commuted the death sentence to life imprisonment. Still later, the sentence was reduced to a few years. Lucky Mr. Lee!

"I have always had a feeling," said Mr. Lee, "that I had help from some power greater than gravity."

YOUR LUCKY DAY

A character in David Storey's play *Home* says: "My lucky day's the last Friday with an 'r' in it when the next month doesn't begin later than the following Monday."

What's *your* lucky day? How did you come to decide that?

"OH, WHAT A [LUCKY] FEELING!"

In Japanese, the family name *Toyoda* takes ten strokes to write. The trade name *Toyota* takes eight. In 1937, when the company was being formed, a numerologist advised that 8 was a luckier number than 10, so the world-famous name is now *Toyota*, not *Toyoda*.

"THE LUCK OF MUNCASTER"

"The Luck of Muncaster" is a green cup given by that embattled king of England, Henry VI, to his host, Sir John Pennington (died 1470), after the Battle of Hexham. Along with the gift, the king promised that the

Pennington family would prosper so long as they preserved that cup unbroken in Muncaster Castle.

In those days, when there was "a divinity" about a king, and when a monarch was the Lord's Anointed, such a promise was to be believed. The lucky cup is still preserved in Muncaster Castle. It is only one of hundreds of thousands of objects the world over to which special powers of "bringing luck" are attached.

SOME PROVERBS ABOUT LUCK

Throw a lucky man into the sea, and he will come up with a fish in his mouth. —Arabic

If a horse gets no wild grass, it never becomes fat; it a man gets no luck, he never becomes rich. —Chinese

Luck has but a slender anchorage. —Danish

The Devil's children have the Devil's luck. —English

He that has ill luck gets ill usage. —French

A lucky man always ends as a fool. —German

My right eye itches; some good luck is near. —Greek

There's luck in odd numbers. —Irish

Bad luck comes by pounds and goes away by ounces. —Italian

An ounce of good luck is better than a ton of brains. —Jugoslavian

Against a lucky man even a god has little power. —Latin

Luck is always borrowed, not owned. —Norwegian

If you were born lucky, even your rooster will lay eggs. —Russian

Better to be the lucky man than the lucky man's son. —Scottish

When good luck comes to you, invite her in. —Spanish

Luck never gives: it lends. —Swedish

Good luck comes to the saucy and the bold. —Welsh

And three more (for good luck) to make twenty:

He who is lucky in love should never play cards.   —Italian

It is better that the luck seek the man than that the man seek the luck.   —Yiddish

The only thing you have to worry about is bad luck. I never have bad luck.   —Harry S Truman

That last quotation was not a proverb. But may I wish that *you* will be able to say it for yourself?

10

Dreams

I'LL SEE YOU IN MY DREAMS

Many superstitious people believe that in dreams they are told of the future or are otherwise in touch with the occult.

This goes beyond the belief that one can compose poetry in dreams or get bright ideas of other sorts in sleep. (James Bovey, a seventeenth-century Englishman—whose descendants, like himself, have held the post of verderer of Exmoor forest—slept for more than forty years with a candle, pen, and paper by his bedside so he could wake up and jot down his thoughts.) Actually we all "process" the information of the day as the night goes by. Artists often use the dream state to get in touch with their unconscious and do some of their best work asleep. Architect Inigo Jones once claimed that he had designed the entrance hall of a manor house after the classical style by dreaming he was in a law court of ancient Rome and then waking up to sketch it quickly.

Ravanalona, queen of Madagascar, executed any of her subjects bold enough to appear uninvited in her dreams. Tippoo Sahib, the ferocious maharajah of Mysore, India, declared that his dreams were official acts of the government; while he ruled (1753–1799) he had each of them recorded in letters of gold. His most colorful superstition, however, may be enshrined in the statue of a tiger eating a British soldier, now in the Victoria and Albert Museum in London. It once had a machine inside that animated it and produced blood-curdling roars and screams. Perhaps it was a mere toy; perhaps it was intended by sympathetic magic to bring disaster on the

143

British troops. If so, it failed; they finally conquered his wonderful capital of Seringapatam and destroyed its treasures—and him.

THE SHAPE OF THINGS TO COME

Beginning a year before the outbreak of World War I, Carl Jung began to have premonitory dreams. An early one was of "a monstrous flood covering all the northern and low-lying lands between the North Sea and the Alps . . . a frightful catastrophe" and a sort of voice-over said: "Look at it well; it is wholly real. . . ."

He continued with daydreams or "controlled hallucinations" that revealed to him a terrible international warfare and (in a dream he shot Wagner's hero Siegfried) even the enemy, Germany. He concluded that "there are things in the psyche which I do not produce" and that in dreams and visions we are spoken to by mysterious outside forces.

"IT CAME TO ME AS IN A DREAM. . . ."

Dreams have produced literary works (such as Coleridge's "Kubla Khan" and Stevenson's *Dr. Jekyll and Mr. Hyde*), even scientific discoveries (such as Watt's inspiration for making perfectly round shot pellets by dropping molten lead from a considerable height into water).

One dream was less happy. A poor Cheshire plowboy named Robert Nixon predicted the Battle of Bosworth Field and its history-changing outcome. The victorious Henry VII heard of this and summoned Nixon to court, entertained him, questioned him, and commanded that (since the lad was illiterate) someone should follow him everywhere, ready at a moment's notice to record any predictions Nixon should make.

One day Nixon predicted he would starve to death. He had had a vivid dream; he was certain it was true.

The king pooh-poohed the idea. A special court officer was charged with the responsibility for the boy's welfare. Now Nixon had nothing to worry about.

When the king was off on business somewhere, the court official (fearing what would happen to himself if any harm came to Nixon) had Nixon locked in a secure room for safekeeping. He retained the only key. Then he was called away on business and departed, taking the key with him.

Robert Nixon, locked in the room, could not be reached. He starved to death. It was as he had predicted.

ONE MAN'S MEDE IS ANOTHER MAN'S PERSIAN

The magi (from whose name comes our word *magic*) read the future for the Medes in astrology and in the livers of sacrificed animals.

When Astyages, the Median ruler, dreamed that his daughter (Mandane) urinated so great a flood that it engulfed all Asia, the wise men took this to mean that from her loins would come the new ruler of all the East. So Astyages married her off to Cambyses, king of Persia, whom he felt sure he could control as a satrap.

Then Astyages (who had a lot of dreams an analyst would welcome) dreamed that from the loins of Mandane a great vine spread to entwine all Asia. The magi decided this signified that the offspring of Mandane and Cambyses would conquer the Medes.

Legend says that therefore the child was (like Oedipus) rejected by his parents and given to a shepherd to be killed; the shepherd in both cases could not bring himself to do the dirty deed, and so the child grew up and made his way to the throne.

The child of Mandane and Cambyses was Cyrus the Great, founder of the Persian empire, who died, after a glorious reign, in 529 B.C.

Historical evidence convinces us now that Herodotus' story of Cyrus (and far different stories in Xenophon's *Cyropaediä*) are mere fantasy. But the ancients' reliance on dreams and oneiromancy was absolutely real.

THE NUMBERS

A great many people who "play the numbers" or want a "lucky number" for some other reason, rely upon their dreams to supply them.

Of course, if you dream of a number itself, you can use that. But be careful. We all know the story of the person whose dream was full of 7s, and so he ran out the next day and bet a bundle on the seventh horse in the seventh race. It came in seventh.

Whatever you dream of can be translated into a number. The method is a little complicated, so pay attention. First, look at this:

1 2 3 4 5 6 7 8 9

A B C D E F G H I

J K L M N O P Q R

S T U V W X Y Z

Let's suppose the main feature of your dream was a car, specifically a Honda. You can work with the three-letter *car* or the five-letter *Honda*.

H O N D A
8 6 5 4 1

Add each pair of numbers: $8 + 6 = 14$
$6 + 5 = 11$
$5 + 4 = 9$
$4 + 1 = 5$

With two digits, take only the last (*i.e.*, 14 gives you 4, 11 gives you 1). Now your five-letter word has given you a four-digit number: 4195. For a three-digit number, add pairs: $4 + 1 = 5$, $1 + 9 = 10$ (take second digit, 0), $9 + 5 = 14$ (make this 4). Your three-digit number is 504. For a two-digit number you will have to regard the 0 as a 1. Thus, $5 + 1 = 6$, $1 + 4 = 5$, result 65. For a 1 digit number, $6 + 5 = 11$, that is 1.

So your numbers are 4195, 504, 65 (some systems would make this 54—but you can always bet on both), and 1.

If you use *car*, you get 319, 41, and 5.

And if your numbers don't win, you may have chosen the wrong feature of your dream to emphasize.

BEAUTIFUL DREAMER, AWAKE UNTO YOURSELF

Virgil's *Aeneid*, in which a dream warned Aeneas of the imminent fall of Troy, is but one example from literature of what many claim to be true in life: that dreams give us "information" of use in the waking world.

Alfred Vierkandt, the German sociologist, contended that "dreams can reflect a sort of self-knowledge and unconscious estimation . . . a concentration and unification through which one may satisfy various hopes; a favorable attitude contributes towards success."

While dreams indicating anxiety or guilt are common (dreams of dying, flying, falling, pursuit, embarrassment at nudity, and so on), they can also bring premonitions. Most of us have numerous premonitions; the trouble is that few of them are correct. Some people claim to have a much better batting average than most of us.

Saint Augustine remarked that even a saint could not be responsible for his dreams. Saint Thomas Aquinas asserted that witches could have dreams sent by the Devil; today we might say they come from the darker side of our personalities, what Jung might call "the other face of God."

Dreaming is, after all, just another altered state, and in such states (trances, hallucinations, mystical visions, or drug-induced states) some people have found revelations. Witches used "magical ointments" to produce such states, in some of which they "flew to the sabbat," or had, or seemed to have, similar strange experiences.

Today scientific research into dreams is extensive and constantly revealing more to us about the nature and function of mind. But even unscientific analysis of your dreams, whether you use one of the common dream books (in which symbolism is explained, sometimes capriciously, sometimes with some accuracy) or not, may tell you more of your inner life.

WARNING

Whether, like a Hopi, you dance your way into *ahola* (possession by spirits of the dead), or like a dervish whirl yourself into ecstasy, whether you burn aconite and henbane or other hallucinogenic substances on your magic altar or ingest chemicals to open "the doors of perception" (as Aldous Huxley so aptly put it), whether you induce trance in yourself or hypnotize others—remember that in some languages *mind* and *soul* are the same and that you would be ill-advised to give up your sanity or your immortal soul. Whom the gods would destroy, they first make mad.

Charles Baudelaire was even leery of sleep, "that sinister adventure of all our nights," for "men go to bed daily with an audacity that would be incomprehensible if we did not know that it is the result of ignorance of the danger."

We forbear to mention what magicians believe about the dangers of sleep lest it keep you awake at night. Happy dreams!

"IN DREAMS BEGIN RESPONSIBILITIES"

In sleep every one of us, every night, experiences those "levels of consciousness" and "mind alteration" that have been so much the subject of interest of late, as we learn that the world's "reality" (as well as the human mind) has two hemispheres.

Experiments in sleep laboratories have shown that a dreamer can be influenced in what he dreams by telepathic transmission from another room. The "sender" stares at a picture, the dreamer somehow "picks it up" as a psychic suggestion. It is therefore not wholly beyond the bounds of possibility that, when we are asleep, we are somehow able to tune into strong signals from people in distress at a distance, able to "receive" veridical dreams.

Thomas King signed on as a member of the crew of the *Isidore* (out of Kennebunkport, Maine, 1847), but refused to sail, because in a dream he had "seen" the ship wrecked and seven of the crew lying dead on the deck. The ship actually was wrecked, and eight of its crew of fifteen disappeared; the remaining seven were corpses on the deck when it was found, which made King's story remarkable.

On the eve of the sailing of the *Amazon* from Port Talbot, Wales, in 1930, the captain had a premonition; he toasted his "last voyage." (Sailors *never* do that!) He sailed, the *Amazon* was hit by a cyclone, and that was the end of her and all who sailed in her. Perhaps, had the "warning" come in a vivid dream, the captain would have been dissuaded from sailing, and all would have been saved.

When one has a dream of disaster, has one seen what will be, or what must be, or what might be? What use is a warning if it cannot ward off calamity? On the other hand, if certain actions are taken to avoid the circumstances of the dream, thereby obviating the disaster, was the dream thus not a true one?

The files of the Society for Psychical Research in London and similar organizations around the world are full of testimony to dreams of prophecy, announcing the death of a loved one at a distance (in India, for example, in Victorian days). People claim they saw the departing person in their dreams or even "awoke" to find him in the room. How many such premonitions turned out to be groundless we shall never know, but we do have documentation for many cases in which the dreams, recorded on waking, eventually were "authenticated."

As some psychics can "see" lost persons in trance and lead police to the bodies, so some people can dream this sort of thing. Mrs. Rhoda Wheeler of La Pointe, Wisconsin, had a dream which guided rescuers to a remote island in Lake Superior on which her clergyman husband and two Indians had been wrecked, which suggests that when we are "dead to the world" we may, some of us, on occasion, be alive to Something Else.

John Chapman, a poor peddler of Swaffham, England, journeyed to London because a dream told him he would find buried treasure there. A stranger whom he stopped to ask directions scoffed at his story and, without knowing who the peddler was, added, "If I believed in dreams, I would be on my way to Swaffham because *I* dreamed there is a treasure buried there in the garden of a man named Chapman."

Chapman turned around, went home, dug up his garden, and found two crocks of treasure. Do you think, had he gone there, he might have found more or less in London?

Another true story. In 1845 Robert Barclay, laird of Urie, wanted to sell his ancestral estate. But he could not find the deed granted to his family by Charles II in 1679. An American Quaker, Joseph Hoag, sleeping in the laird's mansion, dreamed he saw an old man enter his bedchamber and place in a closet a title deed. The room, when he woke, had no closet. But on being told of the dream, Barclay stripped off the wallpaper of the bedchamber, pried loose some boards, and discovered an ancient hiding place in which the valuable deed to the estate had lain undisturbed for 166 years.

People are always claiming they bought just one ticket in a lottery, because the number came to them in a dream, and then won. In Scherin, Germany, there's a public fountain in honor of cigar-manufacturer Johannes Muhlenburg. It shows the donor and four seals. That's right, seals. He dreamed of four seals, consulted a "dream book," played the number in a lottery, and won. A recent winner of the New York State Lottery claimed to have picked the winning number in a dream.

But who or what is "sending" the messages, and how is it that only one person seems to "get" the winning number? Are we dealing with coincidence or communication, reception or deception?

THE MAN IN GREEN

It was the night of May 3, 1812, and John Williams, remotely secure in his manorhouse at Redruth in Cornwall, repeatedly dreamed that he saw a small man in a dark green coat shoot the British prime minister in the House of Commons in faraway London.

His dream was more vivid and persistent than any other he had ever had. The next morning he forced his wife and all his friends to listen to the details. He wanted to go to London and warn the prime minister, but everyone told him that would be folly.

On May 10 the prime minister, Spencer Perceval, had exactly the same dream. There he was, in his dream, in the House of Commons, and up came the small man in the dark green coat. When Perceval told *his* wife and friends all about it the next morning, he was able to add a detail that Williams seems to have missed. The little man's dark green coat sported bright brass buttons.

His family tried to dissuade Perceval from attending the House of Commons that day. His wife especially urged him to stay home. But, having told his dream, Perceval felt rather unburdened. Moreover, he was damned if he was going to miss an important sitting of the House just because of some silly dream, however vivid.

Perceval walked through the lobby of the House of Commons; a bushy-haired man he had never seen before leaped out from behind a pillar and shot him dead.

So it is not true at all, as American newspapers and magazines sometimes claim, that no British prime minister has ever been shot. And it is true that the assassin of Spencer Perceval was wearing a dark green coat with bright brass buttons.

A DREAM FROM SAN FRANCISCO

A woman living in London wrote in 1883 to the Society for Psychical Research to report a dream she had had many years before about a Danish teacher she had known who had gone to Mexico City "to improve his position." In the dream he was sitting in her father's San Francisco office and said to her, "You must not come near me. I am dying in Mexico of the sore throat, and I have come to tell your father."

The father did not have the dream, oddly. But on waking the woman told her family and friends about it. The Danish teacher did die in Mexico, it is reported, at the time indicated and of a *sore throat*.

What a pity the young woman did not record her dream with the SPR at the time, instead of years later. Then the "news" from far-off Mexico could have been measured against her report. What a story that would have made!

"I AM *FATED* TO GO"

A clergyman of Salisbury, England, told the SPR in 1884 of a dream he had had "between June, 1855, and June, 1856" that foretold the death of a friend.

In his dream, the man and a friend were "walking the cloisters of Westminster Abbey" when the friend suddenly said "he must go to a particular gravestone." Urged not to do so, he replied, "No, no, I must go, I am *fated* to go," and he "hurried to the stone, and sank through the floor."

On waking, the clergyman mentioned the strange dream to his landlady. Later he received a letter from his brother saying his friend had "died suddenly from a disease of the heart."

But why was the friend so anxious to get into *someone else's* grave?

IN SUMATRA

When the Bataks of Sumatra want camphor, they go to sleep in a special grove and dream where it is.

CHANNELING YOUR DREAMS

For thousands of years people have been trying to program their dreams. There are many rituals people follow even today to dream what they please. The Seroi of Malaysia have a whole system for producing the dreams they want, and tune them in at night almost like cable television.

WORKING IN YOUR SLEEP

People with a problem often say they will "sleep on it." Can we work in our sleep? The story of an English clergyman named Curnock suggests we can.

His problem was deciphering the *Journal* of John Wesley, the founder of Methodism. Like Pepys' diary, it was in code.

In a bookshop the Reverend Mr. Curnock found a Bible with annotations in the same complicated code. He bought the book and brooded over it for days. One night he dreamed he was reading not the code but what cryptographers call the "clear," and he memorized some of it. When he woke, he used what he recalled to break the code. He was then able to decipher the entire *Journal*, which he published in eight volumes (1909–1916).

That's what Curnock says happened. Do you doubt him?

But why did he dream an uncoded page and not the actual solution to the cipher? Here are questions not of magic but of the processing of information in the sleeping mind, for which, as storyteller H. P. Lovecraft writes in *Beyond the Walls of Sleep*, "one certainly ought not to underestimate the gigantic importance of dreams."

DREAMLAND

Goethe wrote that "the objects which had occupied my attention during the day often reappeared at night in connected dreams. On awakening, a new composition, or a portion of one I had already commenced, presented itself to my mind."

Lord Jeffrey (1773–1850) "had a fancy that though he went to bed with his head stuffed with the names, dates, and other details of various [legal] causes, they were all in order in the morning; which he accounted for," testified his biographer, "by saying that during sleep they all crystallized around their proper centres."

If sleep can permit us creative and organizing activities—that is that we "program" or "process" by night the information that comes to the conscious *and the unconscious* mind during the day—it may also permit us to get in touch with powers of the mind that are clairvoyant or to "tune in" with a greater sensitivity to "messages sent" by others.

Science has now established that certain persons with extrasensory powers can influence the thoughts of dreamers and communicate with them from a distance in the same way that receptivity to ESP is increased by hypnosis. Some people therefore believe that if there are "intelligences" around that are not human and alive—the spirits of the dead, for example, or demons—they may be able to "speak" to us in dreams of things beyond our time and place.

But it usually turns out that people say, "Oh, I had a dream that foretold that exactly" *after* the event. Let's see if we can't get some of these veridical dreams reliably on record. People have often trained themselves to wake up and jot down all the details of their dreams, and certain famous persons have been known to keep pencil and paper by their bedsides for this purpose. Why not write down all the "messages" you receive as "night letters" and see what percentage are accurate?

MERE COINCIDENCE?

G. N. M. Tyrrell in *The Personality of Man* (1947) relates two dreams with remarkable details in common:

On the 7th October, 1938, Monsieur X (the real names are all known) attended a reception at the house of Madame Y in Brussels. He left at 10:30 pm. The same night Madame Y had the following dream: She is at the railway station with a gentleman (unknown); several friends see her off, including Monsieur X. Suddenly the train starts and Madame Y leaves without having time to take all her luggage. She calls through the open window to Monsieur X: 'Please bring my luggage and don't forget the yellow suitcase.' Arrived at her destination, she goes upstairs to the luggage depôt and finds all her luggage except the yellow suitcase. Monsieur X is there, too, and the lady severely rebukes him for his negligence.

The next morning, 8th October, 1938, Madame Y related her dream to a witness, Monsieur Z: and an hour or so afterwards, while Monsieur Z was still present, Monsieur X arrived and before anything was said to him about Madame Y's dream, he recounted his own dream of the previous night, which was as follows: He finds himself at a station and in charge of Madame Y's luggage. A yellow suitcase is specially recommended to his care. He transports all this with great pains, but the yellow suitcase is somehow lost. He mounts the stairs to the luggage depôt and there meets Madame Y. She gives him a severe scolding for his bad behavior.

Your local gypsy would tell you (or you could ask your psychoanalyst) that the loss of something indicates frustration in love, just as walking up the stairs indicates a desire for sexual intercourse and the scolding dissatisfaction with a poor performance. Monsieur X seems to have been able to "deliver" everything but the yellow suitcase (Madame Y's orgasm). Both X and Y seem to have a one-track mind with a single train of thought running on it.

AND IF YOU DREAM ABOUT . . .

Your mind is running on sex if any or (God forbid) all of the following occur in your dreams: driving an automobile, boxes, caves, daggers, elephants, fires, goats, riding a horse, icicles, journeys, knives, locks, machine guns, nudity, orgies, peaches, angry queens, reptiles, snakes, torture, umbrellas, volcanoes, worms, X rays, yellow, zoos.

It is unlucky to dream about accidents, accordions, accusations, acrobats, alligators, altars, ants, fallen apples, automobile accidents, dull axes. . . . That's only the A's.

If you dream of bats, look out. If you dream of cherries, try to eat them. If you dream of a door, try to open it. If you dream of games, try to win. If you dream of paintings, don't buy them in your dream. If you dream of stairs, walk up and never down them. If you dream of water, wake up and get a drink; you are thirsty.

CHEMICAL REACTION

Friedrich August Kekulé von Stradonitz (1829–1896) made a major contribution to organic chemistry by working out the cyclic structure of benzene. In a dream "one of the snakes seized its own tail and the image whirled scornfully before my eyes. As though from a flash of lightning I awoke." By Jove, he had it! The benzene ring!

"PRINCE OF PHYSICIANS NEXT TO HIPPOCRATES"

That was the title given to Galen (c. 129–199), friend and physician to the Emperor Marcus Aurelius, a man so influential that he was still being quoted at the beginning of the Renaissance. He named many bones and muscles with names still used today, and some of his treatments are still in use, though we have given up some of his ideas about the Four Elements and discovered (in the Renaissance) that he was wrong in suggesting that the anatomy of the pig was so like man's that it was unnecessary to cut up human cadavers for study.

Strangely, though Galen was so skilled at diagnosing diseases that he preferred for the patient to remain silent and let him discover all symptoms himself, he liked people to describe their dreams to him in detail, for from that he could tell the future.

APOLLONIUS OF TYANA

The details of Apollonius' life (first century A.D.) are debatable because his biographers did not set to work until he was dead. But it is pretty clear that Apollonius was a miracle worker—he walked through closed doors, he cast out demons, he raised someone from the dead. According to his disciples, he also rose from the dead himself and ascended bodily into heaven.

Among his virtues were humility (he wanted to live simply, "have little and desire nothing") and simplicity (offered a great gift by a king, he chose "dried fruit and some bread"). He preached love of our fellow men, vegetarianism, and (according to his third-century biographer) communism. He gave away his wealth and wandered to India and many other places, preaching to every religion that there was but one God behind everything, that we should all be reincarnated, that we must love all God's creations and harm none.

He was by some later admirers said to have received all his wisdom by revelations in dreams and even to have appeared in their dreams after his departure for heaven to instruct and comfort them.

ONEIROMANCY

A brief study of divination by means of dreams was written by the patriarch of Constantinople, Saint Nicephorus, in ninth-century Greek, and among his interpretations were these:

An eagle means that your dream "whether happy or tragic, is a warning come from God."

A cock means "your dream will soon come true"; a fish means bad news for your plans.

Eating new-baked bread means "imminent misfortune"; a present means "imminent success."

Holding a bee means "your hopes will be disappointed"; a wasp means "danger, attacks."

Walking slowly means "success won with difficulty"; walking straight, "triumph."

Meeting a loved one means "a very hopeful augury," the same as eating grapes.

Talking with a king means "your plans will not mature"; kissed by a king means "you will enjoy the benevolence, favor and support of powerful persons."

Burning coals mean "harm at the hands of your enemies."

Flying means "a journey in a foreign land." If your feet are cut off it means a bad trip awaits you.

Holding a book means "you will rise in the world."

Thunder means "unexpected news."

Walking with back bent means "humiliation," on broken shells means "escape from the snares of your enemies."

Milk means "your enemies' plans for your downfall will fail"; a dog bite means the enemies will succeed in doing you some harm.

Eating something sweet means "bitter disappointment"; eating oranges means "illness."

Laughing means "you will cry when you awaken."

A marriage contract means "a change of abode."

Your house falling down means "loss of your worldly goods."

Meeting a eunuch means "success of an enterprise or the realization of a hope."

A wolf yawning means "beware of empty promises."

Saint Nicephorus has many other ideas. Follow his advice and don't dream of eating lettuce, drinking wine, enjoying figs, or cutting your hair. "If you dream you are sitting with no clothes on," he writes, "it means privation." Try to dream of seeing spilt wine or of washing your feet. Both mean "an end to your troubles." A house on fire or a serpent in your bed are "good signs," oddly. Finally, "If you see the skies or the stars are falling, it means great danger," and "If you see yourself dead, your troubles soon will be ended."

THE CABALA

The mystical writings of the Jews hold many secrets of the interpretation of dreams, very intricately worked out. Since every letter of the Hebrew alphabet has a numerological significance in this occult lore, dreams can give you symbols, numbers, predictions. As the stars are to the cabalists magical letters in the heavens, so people and objects in dreams also carry deep significance. The cabala (meaning "secret tradition") came to the West with the Jewish and Arabic scholars. Ever since then there have been commentaries, ranging from the creative to the crackpot. The basic works are the *seferim* (books) of *Yezira* (Creation), *Bahir* (Light), and *Zohar* (Splendor), and we have the authority of Eleazar of Worms (1176–1238) and Christian writers such as the thirteenth-century Raymond Lully of Catalonia, the fifteenth-century Pico della Mirandola of Italy, the sixteenth-century Paracelsus of Switzerland and Cornelius Agrippa of Germany, the sixteenth-century Robert Fludd and the seventeenth-century Henry More of Britain, and many others, for saying that the Cabala is of far greater interest than the Talmud. Certainly it has much more to say about matters mystical and the interpretation of dreams.

Ginsburg's classic of the midnineteenth century, *The Kabbalah*, has been reprinted in our time, and many scholars of the occult have shown extraordinary interest in the divining and other powers of cabalistic writings and commentaries. Give up your "gypsy dream books" and read the Cabala. Then go forth and enjoy wisdom without pride and power without selfishness.

RISE AND SHINE!

The *Brihadaranyaka Upanishad* of the Buddhists of India give this sage advice: "Let no one wake a man brusquely for it is a matter difficult of cure if the soul find not its way back to him."

Now, what happens when the soul leaves the body permanently and goes to "that undiscovered country" of afterlife? Read on.

11

The Undiscovered Country

GRAVE MATTERS

Here are some burial customs of the past, unfamiliar perhaps, but not more curious than those of today, which Jessica Mitford wittily derided in *The American Way of Death*.

Prehistoric people equipped their dead with weapons for use in the next life and gave evidence of trying to placate their dead, who frightened them. Ancient Britons placed stone hearts in the graves of misers and piled stones on graves to keep the dead from rising. But some tombs had doors.

The Visigoths buried their king Alaric (died 410) in the bed of a river, mounted on his favorite charger and equipped for battle in the spirit world. By diverting the river Busento in Italy, interring Alaric, and then permitting the river to flow once more in its old channel, they made certain that the grave and its treasures would not be disturbed by looters, a worry that Egyptians often had. The Visigoths took the precaution of killing all the slaves who had diverted the river; thus the burial place was kept a secret. In vampire and witch legends running water is supposed to defeat the evil one, and perhaps there was also some element of this superstition in Alaric's last resting place.

The funerary customs of the Egyptians, who were concerned to keep the body preserved so that it could be resurrected and the spirit and fame of the departed commemorated so that it would not die in human memory have produced lasting monuments in the great Pyramids. Most of them have been looted over the centuries, so that the discovery of an intact burial, even of a minor king such as Tutankhamen, is a great archaeological event. Bits of

158

mummy were used in magical concoctions, and "Egyptian" rites have entered Western witchcraft and sorcery.

One lesser known Egyptian monument is the statue of Zedber, a physician, at Atribis where, for centuries, it was venerated by the Egyptians. Covered with magical inscriptions, it had water poured over it—water which the faithful drank as medicine, believing that some of the dead doctor's powers would somehow cure them still.

The Baganda tribe of Africa preserve the jawbones of all their dead kings, so that they may speak wisdom to succeeding rulers.

Roman Catholics preserve relics of saints and martyrs as aids to devotion. Actual pieces of the dead saint (the skull of Saint Catherine of Siena, still missing the two front teeth she knocked out when "the Devil pushed her down stairs," the arm of Saint Francis Xavier, the head of this or that saint in a portrait reliquary, a bit of this bone or hank of that hair) are "first-class relics." Something the saint owned (and preferably touched often, conferring some of his or her virtue on it) is a "second-class relic." Catholics venerate such objects, believing that the grace and favor of God may be obtained through the intercession of the saint so honored.

In witchcraft a piece of a person (fingernail clippings, a lock of hair, or whatever) can be used to work spells, and objects belonging to people enable "physical mediums" to "receive" information about them and sorcerers to work magic upon them. Even your name is a part of you and can be used in magic. The very names of the dead are invoked for magical power, and graves are robbed for pieces of corpses. Ghouls eat the brains of corpses, but magicians want all sorts of other bits and pieces for nefarious work. Even relics of saints can be used in black magic.

In places in Algeria, the graves of saints are sacrosanct, so secure from depredation that the natives pile all sorts of valuables outside the tombs, even precious firewood, sure that no one would dare steal from such a place.

To protect your grave from witches, plant a rowan tree nearby. To counteract necromancy, bury the dead with crucifixes in their hands. And you have heard that so strong is the old folklore of Charon, the ferryman across the River Styx in the Underworld, that even Christians are (or were) sometimes buried with pennies on their eyes, their fare for the last trip on the Underground. It is recalled in an old saying: "So mean he'd steal the pennies off a dead man's eyes." Maybe you'd better throw a few extra coins into the grave, for inflation.

CHILLING THOUGHT

They say that if you feel a sudden chill, someone is walking over your grave. Of course you can avoid this by arranging to be buried at sea, as one man did who wished to thwart a wife who said she would dance on his grave.

APPOINTMENT IN SAMARRA

In the end, we all wind up dead. I don't suppose you have given much thought this week to how and when you will die, but some people appear to have known, through magic or witchcraft or some other obscure means, when the Great Event was coming for them.

Witness these few examples.

Natalie von Hoyningen of Lechts, Esthonia, went to bed, wrote her will, took her pulse, announced that death was five minutes away, and died right on schedule. François de Moncriff, author of *Histoire des Chats*, told his friends, "Tomorrow morning I shall return your books," and died the next day. Many people in history have known exactly when they were going.

Moritz Arndt (1769–1860), German historian, reported to his publisher that in a dream he had seen his gravestone and on it was inscribed, "Died in his 91st Year." Some twenty-four years later he died; he was then in his ninety-first year.

Jane Garon (1705–1806), a widow of Rothwell, England, was warned in childhood that she would die on her birthday. Every year she spent her birthday anniversary in bed. She died in bed on her one-hundredth birthday.

Nothing like being prepared. Many people have ordered their tombs in advance, but few can have been as thoughtful as the wealthy Roman who had his constructed and decorated with four likenesses of himself: One as he appeared at twenty, one as he looked at forty, one as he looked at sixty, one showing him at eighty. He died in his eightieth year.

When he reached eighty, the Egyptian Amenothes carved a statue of himself and inscribed it: "I have attained the age of eighty and I shall endure until the age of 110." They say he died at 110.

Many people die of fright. Magic and witchcraft have capitalized on that. Isaac D'Israeli tells of a knight condemned to the scaffold. He was blindfolded at the block, but instead of having the ax fall, they threw a bucket of water on him, willing to let him off with disgrace rather than death. No use; he died of shock when the water hit him. People have been known to die of fright when they hear of a voodoo curse put upon them. Sophia, Lady Beresford, born February 23, 1666, dreamed she would die on her forty-seventh birthday. The day came, and she felt much relieved to find herself still around—until she realized that she had in error consulted the wrong calendar. She died of shock. It was February 23, 1713.

THE BRIDE WORE BLACK

In my family's papers of the last century, I have found many pieces of writing paper, calling cards, and such, edged in black. There were elaborate rules, too, about how long each member of the family had to wear full mourning or lesser black, gray, or violet. A great-grandmother of mine was in mourning when she got married, so of course her wedding gown was black. Of course it's bad luck to be married in black.

CHINESE FUNERALS

One of the most striking features of the extremely colorful funerals of the Chinese is the use of Hell Money. Scattered along the routes of funeral processions, Hell Money has the same purpose as the clashing gongs and other loud noises (such as firecrackers and music) that accompany these rites. It is hoped that the Hell Money will distract the nearby demons. If they stop to pick up the counterfeit cash, they will ignore the corpse. You can also burn counterfeit money; demons can't tell that your sacrifice is not real, and in this way the very poor can also afford to distract and dispel evil ones.

Those who die by misadventure or violence are watched with special care by the Chinese lest they rise from the grave on the seventh day for revenge.

POT LUCK

Among the Ashanti an *abusua kuruwa* ("family pot") is made when a person dies. Into it goes the hair shaved in mourning by all blood relatives;

then the pot is placed in a special "place of the pots" with cooking pots, hearthstone, and food. Only men are permitted to make these funeral pots and to decorate them with special anthropomorphic and zoomorphic designs. The women make all the other kinds of pots the tribe needs.

FOOD FOR THE DEAD

Some sorcery depends upon offering the dead something they want from the world of the living or performing some service they left undone. Among some African people, "soul pots" are made to resemble departed parents, which their children dutifully fill. In Britain it used to be a custom to leave food in graveyards, at crossroads, and other places for the dead. Hungry but live persons may well have eaten this food (though there were curses to fear if one did so), and this would strengthen the belief of the food givers that the dead were truly present.

THE END

Soldiers used to yearn to die not in bed but "with their boots on." Hindus are also not supposed to die in bed but on the ground, preferably by running water. The Hindus say that to die any other way is unlucky.

ZOMBIES

To most people zombies are powerful cocktails calculated to make you stagger around only partly aware of the world. But the name comes from the "dead" who are supposed to do that in Haiti.

One expert writes:

The Zombie is a dead person whom a sorcerer has taken from the tomb in order to make him, by means of magical powers, seem a living person, making of him a walking cadaver, an automaton of flesh freed from putrefaction, a living dead man.

First, the zombie maker must make a pact with *bakas* (spirits) who serve Baron Saturday (as the Devil is called) to help him. Then he chooses his victim. Riding backward to the victim's house, the *houngan* (sorcerer) sucks out the soul of the victim through the keyhole of the door and breathes it into a bottle. The victim wastes away. The victim dies.

When the victim is buried, the *houngan* steals the corpse from the tomb, assisted by Baron Saturday himself in the guise of an old man with a long white beard. The Devil is conjured up with incantations and put back to rest with more spells (none of which I think you ought to have) and a shower of acacia leaves. It doesn't work, they report in Haiti, unless the body is taken from the grave with chants of "*Mortoo tombo mivi*" ("The dead in the tomb are mine").

Now you have the body obtained in the right way. You must take it past its former residence. If the corpse does not revive and recognize it, everything is going well. Then you can release the soul from the bottle and reinsert it in the body. A powerful drink, and the corpse will revive, now a living dead man, not an independent vampire but the slave of his zombie master.

In this you may perceive a mixture of medieval necromancy and Congolese witchcraft. In Haiti even to this day zombies are believed in, and there is hardly anyone who will not tell you he has seen a zombie or has a friend who has seen one.

What are they? Drugged workers? Or the Baron's *braceros*?

A MEMORY OF THE WIZARD

The zombies and the soul in a bottle reminds me of the souvenir of Thomas Alva Edison. When he died (1931) they did not want his death mask or a lock of his hair. They collected his dying breath in a bottle.

Had Edison not been in a coma, he would probably have had a good laugh over this. On his death his desk was sealed. About fifteen years later, while radio broadcast the great event, it was solemnly opened by his son and found to contain a few pieces of junk and a lot of jokes.

Edison's son had to pass over slip after slip of paper until he could find a joke suitable to be read on the air. Finally Charles Edison found one: "When down in the mouth, remember Jonah. He came out all right."

So much for the Wizard of Menlo Park's "last word."

GOOD INFLUENCE

Parents naturally want good influences on their children. Philip II of Spain stands out. His son Don Carlos was insane; he liked dwarfs, plotting, roasting rabbits alive. His viciousness and violence worried the old man so much that the king ordered that Don Carlos be put to bed with a pious cook. The hope was that some of the piety might rub off on him.

The cook, though pious, was dead, and the scheme failed miserably.

Ultimately the prince was imprisoned for plotting his father's death and died there, possibly murdered at age twenty-three.

IF YOU BELIEVE IN REINCARNATION,
DON'T BE NICE TO PEOPLE

Most people rather like the idea of reincarnation, but whether we come back to earth in some form or hover about out there somewhere is hotly debated, even in spiritualist circles. Do you want your own self to persist or would you prefer a whole new you?

"I expect to pass through the world but once," commented Quaker Stephen Grellet (1773–1855), whereas another philosophical mind has noted that once is enough if you play your cards right. But for some people once is not enough, and they are convinced that they have had a series of past lives. None seems to have been a medieval serf, only a knight or lady, not a housemaid in ancient Egypt, only Cleopatra. Didn't *anybody* work in the Renaissance equivalent of McDonald's? Or do people like that never come back?

J. J. Morse, a spiritualist, certainly believed in the Next World. He used to write "from dictation" the teachings of Tien Sien Tie, a Chinese sage who has not been around since the sixteenth century. But reincarnation? Silly, he said. Otherwise the doctrine of *karma* (reincarnation to atone for the mistakes made in a past life) would make it totally illogical for us to do anything to alleviate human suffering.

"A TIDE IN THE AFFAIRS OF MEN. . . ."

Tennyson dictated that when his poetry was published in collected form the volume should end with the poem "Crossing the Bar," in which he speaks of meeting his "Pilot face to face" and going "out to sea" at death. In Dickens's *David Copperfield*, Barkis at last dies: "And, it being low water, he went out with the tide."

Behind all this is an ancient British superstition that life goes out on the ebb tide, a superstition of which magical ceremonies make some use.

Others believe that most people die at about that dead hour which F. Scott Fitzgerald was fond of saying was "the dark night of the soul," about "three o'clock in the morning."

I had a great-aunt whose theory was that you don't die as long as you will to "hang on," and you go when you have "had enough" (she gave up cheerfully at the age of 106). If there is indeed a psychological factor in staying alive, you can see how strengthening a person's will or weakening a person's confidence can affect life and death.

So all of us, with faith and determination, may be able to summon up the strength to prolong the greatest miracle we know—being a live human being.

DEAD WRONG AND DEAD RIGHT

If a live human being is a miracle, a dead one is a mystery. A corpse makes every thinking person consider at least a little the great question that made Gautama into the Buddha ("the Enlightened One"). What is life and what is its purpose, what is death and what is its purpose?

The corpse of Nicholas L'Hoste, a French spy who drowned himself in the Marne when he saw escape was otherwise impossible, was embalmed, put on trial, convicted, and publicly quartered by being tied to four horses. The corpses of French kings were dug up and thrown around by Revolutionaries. Vindictive people, the French.

The corpses of Constantine the Great and Jeremy Bentham, however, prove that the French are not uniquely morbid.

Constantine the Great's corpse ruled the Roman empire for three months. It was preserved, sat on the throne, and was "consulted" daily by government officials until the emperor's son and successor got home from Constantinople.

Jeremy Bentham was an English expert on jurisprudence and ethics, one of the most able writers on utilitarianism. He was a rather long-winded stylist (Edward FitzGerald wondered "what would have happened to Christianity if Jeremy Bentham had been given the writing of the Parables") and has been, in a sort of way, a rather long-lived official of the University of London. Though he died in 1832, he still attends official meetings. He is recorded as "present but not voting." His preserved body is wheeled up to the conference table, hat and stick and all, gruesomely lifelike. When he is not attending meetings, they keep him in a sort of closet. You can see him to this day in London.

Those who live on, whether using a part of a corpse or the whole thing, often violate what may be called the privacy of the dead.

THE BLACK LACE PILLOW

In these days when doctors and relatives are empowered to "pull the plug" on brain-dead patients, it is probably not difficult to understand the feelings of our ancestors who, for selfish, practical, or humanitarian reasons, were moved to help the dying get there faster.

Many were the devices employed to speed up the inevitable. Some were thought magical. One of these was a pillow, covered in black lace, purported to have been made by a nun of Ely, England, and handed down from generation to generation to help bring quicker death to a suffering soul.

Placed beneath the head of a dying person, it was suddenly whipped out, giving him or her (it was hoped) a nasty shock, hastening them the way that they were going. Just seeing it arrive in the sickroom must have been less than fortifying.

In 1902 the last old lady who owned and operated this device passed on (without its assistance), and that was the end of the black lace pillow.

HEADS OF STATE

Because it contains the brain and hence the personality, the head has long been regarded as the most likely part of the body to retain some of the spirit of the deceased. Hence head hunters and shrinkers and scalp takers.

A severed head—I mentioned that of Saint Catherine of Siena earlier—can be seen in many European collections of relics. You used to be able to see the heads of traitors stuck up on London Bridge or Micklegate Bar in York, left until they rotted to nothingness or were stolen.

There are two heads of Saint Thomas Aquinas, and a dispute has raged for centuries over which is the real one. The same fate befell Button Gwinnett (1735–77), signer of the Declaration for Georgia (whose chief claim to fame is that his signature is the rarest of all Signers' signatures—he died so young and so obscurely that he had few chances to sign anything). Sir Thomas More's daughter treasured his severed head, as well she might. He made a brave, even jaunty end, mounting the scaffold for his faith and telling the headsman, "Assist me up, and in coming down, I will shift for myself." The daughter subsequently carried the head with her everywhere. Like Juana the Mad of Spain, who brought her dead husband entire wherever she was invited, asking the young More daughter to a party put something of a damper on jollity.

At the end of Shakespeare's play, Macbeth's head is supposed to be brought on stage on a pole, but directors often omit this. The head of Oliver Cromwell was dug up at the Restoration (1660) and used as a football by the Royalists. Its exact place of burial is now a secret, to prevent further outrages. Last seen officially on top of Westminster Hall, Cromwell's head was blown down in a gale, picked up by a sentry, and sold, passing through various hands (including those of "a drunken and dissolute actor called Samuel Russell," a Canon Wilkinson, and Sidney Sussex College—Cromwell's own college—at Cambridge). When the head was reburied in 1960, the memorial was not exactly placed, and the secret resting place is presumably safe.

Few corpses have suffered the indignities of Cromwell's, which was even tied to a hurdle, though largely decomposed, dragged to Tyburn, and hanged. Before that it rested a night at the Red Lion inn in Holborn, giving rise to a tradition that Cromwell's ghost haunts that spot.

A head, supposedly of the duke of Suffolk, father of the tragic "nine days' queen," Lady Jane Grey, was found, 247 years after Suffolk's beheading, in the vault of Holy Trinity Church in London; oak sawdust from the scaffold, they said, had perfectly preserved it.

Head stealing was not unheard of in the heyday of sorcery. If necromancers did not want to raise the whole body from the dead they might try to make the head speak. To do this, one takes the head of a murdered eldest son, opens it, applies ammonia and oil, and places an amulet of virgin gold under the tongue. Charles IX of France, who in 1560 at the age of ten became king under the regency of his mother (the redoubtable Catherine de Médicis), had one of these made for him. He had "a young Jew" murdered for the purpose.

Several magicians, including the thirteenth-century Franciscan and alchemist Roger Bacon, were supposed to have made neater, more durable speaking heads out of brass.

TOWERS OF SILENCE

The Parsees (originally from Persia) in India have such respect for the sacredness of the earth that they shrink from defiling it even with the dead bodies of their loved ones. They take their dead to the Towers of Silence in Bombay. There they are exposed to the vultures, who pick the bones clean.

In Western tradition seldom or never does a ghost appear as a skeleton, while the ghosts of those cremated (an increasingly popular practice although forbidden by a number of religions) are practically never seen.

"I'M MY OWN GRANDPA!"

Jess Stern in *Yoga, Youth and Reincarnation* (1968) refers to the "regression" under hypnosis of a man in Wilmington, Delaware, who believed in reincarnation and who seemed to recall being in another body at the time of the Spanish-American War. He had other odd feelings. "He couldn't understand why he was so anxiously following the romance of his son and a pretty girl friend." And he heaved a sigh of relief when the son finally married the girl. Why? Because "he was slated to return as his own [great-]grandson, so he was in a sense waiting for his own father to materialize."

In magical circles people often claim to be the reincarnation of an earlier magician, say Paracelsus or Cornelius Agrippa (who, despite their classical-sounding names, were sixteenth-century physician/occultists), or even to have gone on living generation after generation (like the Comte de Saint-Germain). But I have never seen another case of one believing he was his own ancestor.

BAPTIZING THE DEAD

Joseph Smith said that the living could be baptized in the Mormon religion in the name of those who had died before that dispensation.

His authority was not so much the Angel Moroni (whom he encountered in New York) as I Peter 3:18–20, which speaks of Jesus preaching to the spirits of the dead, and I Corinthians 15:29, where Saint Paul writes of vicarious baptism for the departed. Other Christian sects have read these texts differently.

The Mormon desire to "seek out the dead" and posthumously bring relatives into the fold has led the Church of Latter-Day Saints to build up perhaps the most extensive genealogical archives in the history of the world and to baptize in the Mormon temple in Salt Lake City such non-Mormons as Abraham Lincoln.

One cannot say, of course, whether any of those offered this postmortem opportunity have availed themselves of it. In the end, the choice is theirs.

Baptism has been important in other religions, of course, and in witchcraft as well, where unbaptized infants were eagerly sought. The Devil's brood were baptized in his name. A baptized animal if sacrificed was supposed to grant certain powers of evil. But nobody ever thought of *un*baptizing the dead to bring them to the Devil's Party.

FUNERALS FOR THE LIVING

The Greek philosopher Diogenes one day told his followers that, when he died, he wished not to be buried with ceremony but to be left exposed to the sun and rain. That, he said, would consume his body.

But, they objected, the dogs would tear to pieces an unburied corpse.

"Then you must put a stick in my hands," replied Diogenes, "that I may drive them away."

"But when you are dead you will neither see nor feel anything."

"You see what fools you are," replied Diogenes; "for if that be the case, what matters it by what I am devoured, or what becomes of me when I shall be insensible to everything?"

Funerals cannot matter much to the dead; they are chiefly for the living. Faced with death, people need to mark and mourn the occasion, and even the most agnostic may want some comfort from ceremony or the most sophisticated some allaying of deep-seated old fears and superstitions.

Few of us can say with equanimity what Lt. Gen. Henry Hawley (died March 24, 1759) said: "My carcass may be put anywhere; it is equal to me, but I will have no more expense or ridiculous show, than if a poor soldier (who is as good a man) were to be buried. . . . The priest, I conclude, will have his fee—let the puppy have it. Pay the carpenter for the carcass-box."

Death, whether it is annihilation or entry into another kind of existence, is an occasion, and the feelings that have always struck the living at that time have provided a great deal of the impetus for occult beliefs and practices. Even a belief in demons is, in a way, comforting; if they exist, this is not "the be all and the end all here." Hardly anyone wants to be a ghost (certainly not immediately), but however frightening the idea of ghosts may be, it is also fundamentally a comfort.

CENOTAPH

Providing some sort of memorial for the dead so that a spirit may not be homeless in the afterlife has long been a concern of the living. Making some gesture to bury her brother (which her uncle has forbidden) is a strong motivation for Antigone in Sophocles' play of that title.

World wars have sentimentally but successfully provided graves for various "unknown soldiers," some nations choosing to erect cenotaphs (tombs in which no body is buried). France and America each chose an unidentified corpse and interred it in state in their respective capitals. At Runnymede, where King John sealed the Magna Carta, is a monument by Sir Edward Maufe to the air forces of the Commonwealth, remembering all those whose graves are unknown. Around the world are many monuments to persons lost at sea, and pagan custom is combined with modern sentiment when flowers are thrown into the water to memorialize deaths at sea.

REST IN PEACE

Flowers from the earliest times may have been placed on the bodies of the dead for sentimental as well as practical purposes (in days before embalming). Flowers are perfect symbols of beauty that perishes. They may also in a sense represent gifts to the dead, and it is impossible to say exactly to what extent gifts were offered to the dead to placate them, to protect the living against them. In magic and witchcraft we preserve our very ambiguous attitude toward the dead. We try to guard against them and, if possible, to use them for our benefit. We mourn them and we fear them. We give the dead homes to please them, to honor them, and to hold them.

We like to think of the dead as sleeping, and we do not like to think of what might happen if they are aroused from that "sleep." We are especially fearful and revolted in regard to grave robbers, but from the earliest times graves have been violated, generally to steal treasures entombed with the dead. Treasure hunters evaded all the ingenious protections provided by the Egyptian architects and desecrated the tombs of the pharaohs before archaeologists could get there to do likewise. In more recent times, "resurrectionists" stole bodies to sell to anatomists. The corpse of Laurence Sterne, for instance, was stolen only two days after his death (in 1768) by grave robbers, so a tombstone now marks the empty grave of the immortal author of *Tristram Shandy*. Mummies of pharaohs and kings have been unceremoniously dumped out of their coffins to be put on display in museums. Shakespeare has so far escaped this indignity. His epitaph contains a curse on anyone who dares disturb his "bones," and up to this day it has worked.

BODY OF KNOWLEDGE

Today death is hidden from us as much as possible. Family and friends seldom gather to watch a loved one die, as they used to. Today the "loved one" is quickly consigned to the "mortician," and the "cosmetician" begins his work (if the body is to be displayed, though increasingly the lid of the coffin is closed). At the funeral, the coffin is often covered with "floral tributes," so that funerals are getting perilously close to being flower shows. Try as we might to forget it, the dead body is there, in the box. However much we prettify, death is a fact. As faith wanes, we claim less and less knowledge of death's purpose, its nature, its mystery. And, as always, the less knowledge there is, the more fear, and the more fear, the more superstition.

It is alleged that if you touch a corpse, you will have nightmares about it. I do not find this true, but a friend of mine who "shook hands" with the mummified corpse of a "crusader," astoundingly preserved by the dry air in the vaults of St. Michan's, Dublin, had a terrible recurrent dream for a long while afterward. It was "set" in Ireland during the early nineteenth century, so that may not be a "crusader" after all. . . .

They say that if you kiss a corpse you will never be afraid of the dead. I think that probably has to happen in reverse order.

At the wake, drink up. The pallbearers must drink first. Each cup you quaff is supposed to contain some of the sins of the dead, so help the entrance into the next world as much as you can.

"POSSESSION BY GOOD OR EVIL SPIRITS . . ."

You might think that films, with all the photographic tricks available to them, would have brought many ghost stories to the screen, but cinema prefers to deal in more realistic surfaces. There has been a rash of movies about possession.

The popularity of a number of books, often made into movies, about multiple personalities (Eve with three, Sybil with five, others with dozens) prepared the public for what psychologists call "fragmented ego" and what demonologists called "possession," the inhabiting of a body by another intelligence from beyond the mundane world.

Ramona Stewart's novel *The Possession of Joel Delaney* (1972) was a case in point. Joel was possessed by the spirit of one Tonio Perez, a seventeen-year-old Puerto Rican maniac with a love of knives and a penchant for decapitating pretty girls. So his sister sought the help of Don Pedro, who ran the Botánica Santa Barbara and conducted a magical ceremony intended to drive out the evil spirit.

"All you have open is your eyes," he says to Joel's distraught sister. "Are you willing to believe and accept what you are told?" Well, the sister tries, attending a ritual that is a mixture of Christian exorcism and pagan rites. But Joel does not attend in person, and the attempt to drive the spirit of the dead Tonio into one of those at the ceremony (so that it can then be exorcised) apparently fails.

When Joel is shot by police at a beach house, his sister picks up his knife, and as the story ends she seems to have become the new residence of the evil spirit.

Like many other similar tales, *Joel Delaney* was made into a movie. Such films are long on violence and short on explanations, but they are clear evidence that the general public finds "possession" as gripping as did our medieval ancestors.

". . . ALIVE WITH THE SOUND OF MUSIC"

In my Shakespeare studies I have come across some books supposedly dictated by the Bard and his colleagues from Beyond. I have friends who "receive" poetry from Hart Crane and Walt Whitman, too, although death seems to have a deleterious effect upon talent.

Richard Strauss dedicated a wind serenade to the ghost of Mozart, implying that Wolfgang Amadeus himself had inspired him to compose it, perhaps even helped him from the grave.

Mrs. Rosemary Brown in Britain reported "receiving" compositions from Lizst and others, but an English musical authority describes them as "free association of sounds." If that's really what Lizst, Chopin, and the others are capable of these days, they are better off dead.

VIKINGS!

The many Viking invasions of Western Europe produced both new customs of magic and witchcraft and at the same time a suspicion that the dead in Valhalla might be having too good a time to bother with us.

In case they turned nasty, however, it was wise to propitiate them. Thietmar of Meresburg, a Danish chronicler of the eleventh century, records that in Lejre, Denmark, every nine years there was a Yule festival in January celebrated "by, among other things, sacrificing ninety-nine humans and as many horses to their gods, as well as dogs and cocks, and also hawks." In the sacred grove dedicated to Freya and Thor at Uppsala, Sweden, wrote Adam of Bremen in his chronicle, they also sacrificed every nine years: "Of all living things that are male and female, they offer nine heads." Then the corpses of men, women, and animals festooned the ash trees of the grove.

Peter Brent in *The Viking Saga* identifies sacrifice as "the basic act of worship" in Scandinavia. "What was offered heavenwards included the whole range of objects within mankind's control and gift, for the gods were greedy, capricious and powerful."

Someone should study the history of sacrifice, determine what has been offered to man's gods over the millenia of recorded history, and analyze what this shows about man's conception of his deities and himself. The gods of the Vikings were in their image: brave, proud, audacious, and rapacious.

The Vikings were avid collectors. They would take anything not nailed down. And they did not like the idea of "you can't take it with you." (Moreover, to leave easy riches to your children might make them soft.) When a Viking went, so did his wealth. It was a rule that a third of a man's estate must be spent on drink for those who attended the funeral.

At this grand affair the hero was buried with riches and honors. Sometimes the body was placed on a ship full of treasure and the ship was burned at sea. Sometimes the body was buried on land. Sometimes human sacrifices burned with the hero after they had been ritually murdered. Brent writes that "the killing of a companion for the dead certainly occurred in Norway, Sweden, Iceland and the Isle of Man" and chiefs were likely to be sent to the afterlife with a slave girl, perhaps with their horses.

RESERVED PLACE

The New Jerusalem (Revelations 21:16) is "twelve thousand furlongs," worked out by one authority as 497,793,088,000,000,000,000 cubic feet.

So don't worry about getting in. But if you want a special place the Yezidis, a group of Kurdish-speaking peoples with a religion of their own, will sell you one. Or you can check out with your local clergy about other offers in heavenly dwelling places. Uncertain about the prospects? Better be cautious. As Woody Allen says, "I don't believe in an afterlife, although I am bringing a change of underwear."

OMENS OF DEATH

The occult sciences have long concerned themselves with pulling aside the veil of the future, and astrology, necromancy, fortune-telling, and other superstitious practices have caused occultists to look for signs.

Saint Augustine warned that though all signs are things, not all things are signs. Where to look? Up into the sky or down into the entrails of animals?

Heavenly portents are said to have heralded the death of kings, and the star of Bethlehem announced the birth of the King of Kings. Even lesser mortals have omens to guide them. The bishops of Salisbury, England, keep an eye on the White Birds of Salisbury Plain; when they appear (as when owls bring similar unwelcome messages to the Wardour family of Arundel), death is near. The O'Neills, like many lesser Irish families, have their banshee. If you happen to hear a banshee (and you do not have to be an O'Neill), a sweet crooning sound means you will die peacefully. A malevolent howl means you are in for a much worse end.

YOU CAN GO TO HELL

Clergymen joke about the notice board outside a church: "Do You Know What HELL Is? Come In and Hear Our New Organist."

Whatever Hell is, whether alienation or a crowded prison, "other people" or private suffering, a state of mind or a place of fire and brimstone, the concept has long been with us and contributes much to our vision of the undiscovered country.

You can go to a real Hell (a town in Scandinavia) or Hell Bay (on Bryher, one of the Isles of Scilly). The ancient Greek Hell was entered at Cape Tenaris and Eleusis, the Italian Hell, through a cave at Cumae near Naples. The French said Hell was in the Alpes Maritimes.

In the parish register of St. Nicholas Within the Liberties, Dublin, there is an entry dated May 20, 1735: "Sarah Read from Hell."

"No," comments *Irish Times*, "poor Sarah was no witch, but a very respectable person indeed, and was buried with all Christian dignity. For Hell was the old name of Christ Church Lane, close to the old Law Courts." Similarly, an old street near Westminster Palace Yard was originally named Hell.

BODY AND SOUL

Tennyson rejoiced to think that at his death his spirit would not be a personality any longer but would become part of something larger, what Emerson called the oversoul. Others want to survive as individual personalities after death, freed of the body, and Christians believe in a resurrection of the body, but not necessarily the same body as in this life. "It is sown a natural body," says Paul in I Corinthians, 15:44; "it is raised a spiritual body." The Talmud mentions the Bone of Luz, from which the body was to be restored. For many centuries anatomists hunted in vain for this mystical bone. When they couldn't find it, they theorized that it vaporized at death. It was supposed to depart at death to begin its real work.

Can the spirit leave the body before death, to roam around the world or even just to float up to the ceiling? Some people who have been near death, even technically and momentarily dead, claim they have left their bodies in spirit and watched themselves "down there" for a while before resuming the intimate union.

After death, does the soul hang around or go elsewhere? Is it ill-disposed toward the living, as many people (not all of them primitive) believe? Is it reincarnated? Does it join God? Or what?

Too soon to know for certain.

Index